SPEAK LIKE A
NATIVE

SPEAK LIKE A NATIVE

Professional Secrets for Mastering Foreign Languages

MICHAEL D. JANICH

PALADIN PRESS • BOULDER, COLORADO

Also by Michael D. Janich:

Advanced Fighting Folders (video)
Blowguns
Breath of Death (video)
Fighting Folders
Fighting Folders (video)
Homemade Martial Arts Training Equipment
Knife Fighting
Making It Stick (video)
Mastering Fighting Folders (video)
Mastering the Balisong Knife (video)
Mook Jong Construction Manual
Street Steel

Speak Like a Native:
Professional Secrets for Mastering Foreign Languages
by Michael D. Janich

Copyright © 2004 by Michael D. Janich
ISBN 13: 978-1-58160-452-8
Printed in the United States of America

Published by Paladin Press, a division of
Paladin Enterprises, Inc.
Gunbarrel Tech Center
7077 Winchester Circle
Boulder, Colorado 80301 USA
+1.303.443.7250

Direct inquiries and/or orders to the above address.

PALADIN, PALADIN PRESS, and the "horse head" design
are trademarks belonging to Paladin Enterprises and
registered in United States Patent and Trademark Office.

Visit our Web site at www.paladin-press.com

Table of Contents

PART 2: DEVELOPING A PLAN • 21

Step 1:   Decide on your specific goals and determine how and under what circumstances you will use your language skills.

Step 2:   Research your language to become familiar with its overall organization, structure, and writing system.

Step 3:   Visit your local library and become familiar with the types of materials available on your target language. If you plan on buying language study materials, visit local bookstores, including university bookstores, and see what types of materials are available there and at what cost.

Step 4:   In examining the study materials available to you, pay close attention to the phonetic system used to teach the language. If the writing system of your target language is not a convenient and easily learned phonetic system, the study materials will probably use one or more romanization systems to teach pronunciation. Become familiar with these, try to determine if there is a popular standard, and make the decision to stick with a specific system.

Step 5:   Identify other unique aspects of your target language and assess the challenges they will present to your learning it.

Step 6:   Based on your initial research and your now deeper understanding of your target language, reassess your goals and add, delete, or reprioritize as necessary.

Step 7: Compare the English content of the various study materials you've found with your goals and select the materials that best represent the types of topics you'd like to focus on.

Step 8: Purchase all the administrative supplies you'll need to support your study efforts and keep them organized.

Step 9: Learn the phonetic system of your target language and, if necessary, an associated romanization system.

Step 10: Identify characteristics and nuances of your target language that are critical to its structure and use and get these concepts clear in your head.

Step 11: Using your personalized, prioritized list of goals and objectives, begin your study of the language.

Step 12: After a few study sessions, and after gaining a deeper understanding of your target language, reassess your goals and adjust accordingly.

Dedication

This book is dedicated to Garnett "Bill" Bell, one of the most talented real-world linguists I have ever seen and a true American hero. A decorated Vietnam veteran, Bill was the official interpreter during the return of U.S. prisoners of war at Operation Homecoming in 1973. He later devoted his life to supporting our country's efforts to account for our prisoners of war/missing in action (POW/MIA).

Prior to our normalization of relations with the Socialist Republic of Vietnam, Bill was functionally the senior U.S. statesman for our negotiations with the Vietnamese government. Through his amazing skills as a linguist, interviewer, negotiator, investigator, and analyst, he earned the highest respect of both Vietnamese and American experts and was universally regarded as *the* authority on the POW/MIA issue.

Unfortunately, Bill's knowledge

Garnett "Bill" Bell, linguist warrior extraordinaire.

and abilities were not valued by some members of the U.S. leadership. His commitment to doing the job right and honoring the memories of our missing servicemen was considered an obstacle to their "progress" on the resolution of the issue. Rather than compromise his own standards of excellence, Bill stepped down and continued to support and serve the families of our missing servicemen through his private efforts.

I was extremely fortunate to know and work with Bill during my service with the U.S. government and still stand in awe of his abilities. Through my experiences with him, I learned that language can be a toy, a tool, and a weapon. I also learned a lot about dedication and what it really takes to be the best at something. That he taught me by example.

Thank you, Bill, for everything. Many of us are forever grateful for all you've done.

Introduction

The goal of this book is to provide you, the aspiring language student, with proven study methods and strategies that will accelerate your learning of a foreign language. In addition to making the learning process more effective, I hope to help you define and constantly refine your learning objectives so you can focus on the aspects of language that are most relevant to your needs and interests.

The methods described in this book are based on more than 25 years of experience learning foreign languages—both my own personal experience and the experiences of countless other amateur and professional linguists. What is presented is not theory; it is a distillation of proven methods successfully used by linguists ranging from high school Spanish students to U.S. State Department interpreters.

All the methods in this book have been used effectively and collectively represent one of the most complete and logically structured templates for language study ever assembled, but this book does not possess magical powers. Learning *anything* takes time and effort. Learning languages is no different. The cruel truth is that you are about as likely to become fluent in a language in "a few minutes a day" as you are to lose weight on a cheesecake and beer diet.

If you truly want to learn and use a language, this book will help you define and achieve your goals in a practical, effective, and rational way. The higher you set your goals, the harder you'll have to work and the more this book will help.

For the record, I am a two-time graduate with honors from the Defense Language Institute Foreign Language Center (DLIFLC) in Monterey, California. After completing its basic one-year course in Chinese-Mandarin, I completed intermediate and advanced Chinese training through the National Security Agency (NSA), where I served a three-year tour as a political-military intelligence analyst and translator.

During my second period of study at DLIFLC, I learned Vietnamese. I graduated with one of the highest course averages since the Vietnam War and beat out scores of honor grads in Arabic, Chinese, Korean, Czech, Russian, and other languages to receive the Commandant's Award as the outstanding graduate for my class cycle. I was then assigned to U.S. Army Field Station Kunia in Hawaii, where I worked as a Vietnamese voice intercept operator and analyst. During my four-year tour there, I earned certification as a language transcriber and became only the second U.S. Army Vietnamese linguist to become professionalized as a voice language analyst by NSA's Cryptologic Career Service Professionalization Program.

During my tour in Hawaii, I was selected to support the Joint Casualty Resolution Center (JCRC)—the organiza-

The author's experience as a linguist includes serving as a team leader for POW/MIA investigation teams in Southeast Asia. Here he conducts an interview of a former North Vietnamese officer in Bac Thai Province, northern Vietnam.

tion then responsible for investigating the fates of American POW/MIA from the Vietnam War—and served a six-month tour at the U.S. Embassy in Bangkok, Thailand. While there, I interviewed Vietnamese refugees in camps throughout Thailand regarding POW/MIA information and served as interpreter for a U.S. archaeological team during the excavation of aircraft crash and burial sites in northern Vietnam.

After nine years of military service, I was recruited by the Defense Intelligence Agency (DIA) Stony Beach Program to serve as an intelligence officer in the U.S. consulate in Hong Kong. In that capacity, I debriefed Vietnamese political refugees and economic migrants concerning their knowledge of Americans allegedly captured alive during the Vietnam War and other intelligence collection requirements. My areas of responsibility included the dozen-plus detention centers in the Hong Kong territories and the asylum and refugee resettlement camps in the Philippines.

Following nearly two years of distinguished service in DIA, I transferred to Bangkok to work once again for JCRC, which was shortly thereafter reorganized as the Joint Task Force-Full Accounting (JTF-FA). As the youngest investigation team leader for this organization, I was responsible for leading 8- to 10-man teams during on-site POW/MIA investigations throughout Vietnam. I also served as official interpreter for forensic examination activities in Hanoi and during formal negotiations between representatives of the United States and the government of the Socialist Republic of Vietnam.

After being expelled from Vietnam as part of a Cold War political stunt, I continued to support JTF-FA's collection and analysis by interviewing Vietnamese refugees in Thailand, Singapore, Malaysia, Indonesia, Hong Kong, Macau, and Japan. I also served for more than a year as a senior intelligence analyst and linguist for investigation and forensic recovery teams operating in Laos before resigning from government service.

During my 15 years of government service, I had the opportunity to study Chinese-Mandarin and Vietnamese extensively and apply both languages in both casual and operational contexts. I also lived and traveled extensively in Asia, studying and applying a variety of other languages, including Thai, Lao, Cantonese, Japanese, and Khmer. For the record, I started out studying Spanish in high school, and my wife of 20 years is Hispanic, fluent in Spanish, and a DLIFLC graduate in Korean.

My reason for sharing all this is not to impress you but to give you confidence in the information you will read in this book. I'm no genius, but I've been able to study, learn, and use a number of foreign languages during my life. In the process, I've learned, both through personal experience and through the experiences of countless other linguists, what works and what doesn't when it comes to learning a foreign language. Based on these experiences, I took the best methods and narrowed them further, selecting the ones I feel are critical to all language study, as well as a number of tips and strategies that seem to work best for most people. I then organized these strategies into a logical sequence that will help you understand the nature of your target language, set realistic goals, and achieve those goals in the most efficient way possible.

In this book, you will first learn what I consider to be the 10 *rules* of learning a foreign language. By developing a good understanding and acceptance of these rules, you will be able to begin your study with a proper mind-set and a series of realistic goals and expectations.

The second section of the book presents my 12-step process for learning a foreign language. This process is a series of activities designed to help you understand the nature of your target language, establish your own definition of fluency, assemble the right materials, organize your study, and structure ongoing study programs to achieve your long-term linguistic goals.

Finally, this book shares 50 proven tips and strategies that professional linguists, interpreters, and translators have used to accelerate and enhance their study and application of foreign languages. No matter what your personal linguistic goals may be, these surefire strategies are certain to make your foreign language study more efficient and productive than ever before.

Once again, this book is not a magic pill that will make you fluent overnight. There is no such thing. However, this *is* the book that I wish I'd had years ago when I first started learning a foreign language. If it saves you a few headaches and makes your study of foreign languages a little easier and more enjoyable, I've done my job well.

PART

Getting Organized

Before you can begin studying any language, you need to have at least a basic understanding of what you're getting into. Without an understanding of *what* your target language is, the process of determining *how* to study it is much more difficult.

In this section, I'll get you started on the process of categorizing your target language and help you get organized to study it effectively. We'll also take an honest look at the challenges associated with studying languages and help you embrace the idea that fluency is ultimately defined by *your* goals, not those established by your high school French teacher (whom you didn't like anyway).

As we do this, we'll examine 10 basic rules of language study that I learned the hard way. By understanding and accepting these rules right up front, you will hopefully spare yourself some of the brain cramps I suffered over the years. You will probably also realize that while some of the rules are cruel and unforgiving, others are incredibly liberating and will allow you to pursue your target language on your own terms. As with any discipline, the cruel and unforgiving rules are there for a reason. If you ignore them, you'll probably have more fun, but you won't learn much. If you accept them and deal with them from the start, you'll go a lot further toward becoming a much better linguist.

Rule 1: Learn your own language well before you attempt to learn someone else's.

As strange as it may sound, one of the best things you can do to enhance your ability to learn a foreign language is to first learn your own. Since this book is written in English, I'm assuming that what we're talking about here is the English language.

Now before you get all bunged up because I insulted your intelligence, stop and think about it. How long has it been since you diagrammed a sentence? When was the last time you consciously thought about such things as pronouns, adverbs, adjectives, preterit tenses, and past participles? Have you ever understood the difference between a direct object and an indirect object?

I'm not saying that you need to have a degree in English before you learn another language, but you should at least be familiar with the terminology and the functions of the various parts of speech in your own language before you attempt to tackle them in someone else's. This knowledge is also helpful because in some languages the same linguistic concepts and ideas are expressed in very different ways. When that happens, you'll find that you're not only learning how to translate, but also what *doesn't* translate or typically isn't translated when operating in your new language. That's often the first step toward thinking in your target language—*the* most difficult and productive language study activity you can ever do.

Finally, if you ever plan to study a foreign language in a classroom environment with a nonnative English-speaking instructor, you'll be glad you brushed up on your English grammar. There's nothing quite as demeaning as being lectured on the technicalities of your own language by a nonnative English speaker.

Rule 2: **You only get out what you put in. If you want to converse at a college level in a foreign language, you'd better plan on going to college in a foreign country.**

OK. You're up to speed on the difference between a preposition and a proposition (though both are useful linguistically, they *are* different), so you're ready to learn Spanish in 10 minutes a day, right? Well, maybe. If your idea of learning Spanish is learning a few phrases that will ensure that you can always (a) order a beer and (b) find a bathroom to purge said beer, 10 minutes a day should do it. However, if your concept of learning Spanish means having the ability to discuss critical socioeconomic issues with Mexican government officials, you'd better clear your schedule for a while.

Like anything else in life, how well you speak a language is determined by the context in which you apply your skills. The higher you set your goals, the harder you're going to have to work. Think about it. If you want to converse with a college graduate from a foreign country at *his* education level and in *his* language, you'll need to have studied and practiced his language almost as long and hard as he has. Conversely, if you only want to ask some basic directions, order a meal, and pay your hotel bill, you're operating at a much lower level and can achieve that goal in a much shorter time.

In case you didn't notice, that was the bad news: you only get out what you put in. Contrary to the advertising and hype you'll see with many other language books, audiocassettes, and videos, you cannot master an entire foreign language in 10 minutes a day. It just won't happen.

The farther off the beaten track you go, the higher you should set your linguistic goals. As you might imagine, the odds of finding another English speaker in this rural Lao village are pretty slim.

The good news, however, is the rest of this book, which contains proven techniques and strategies that will allow you to learn and use a foreign language much more effectively than standard study methods. When combined with some special communications skills (read: cheating) that we'll cover later, you'll find that these techniques and study methods will enable you to use a foreign language to get what you want and go where you want more effectively than any other approach to language study.

Rule 3: Success is determined by the goals you set. Establish a series of realistic goals by asking yourself honest questions about how you plan to use the language.

Now that we know that 10 minutes of study a day will not prepare us for political debates in a foreign language, let's look at setting some realistic goals. *Before you begin any program of foreign language study, you must first identify and set practical, achievable goals.* As with any other endeavor, if you aim too high right from the start, you're likely to get discouraged when you don't achieve your lofty goals in a short period. On the other hand, if you set a series of practical, reasonable goals and go about achieving them in a methodical manner, each success will prime you and inspire you for the next.

It is also quite possible that your linguistic goals are simple and finite. If this is the case, your language study could be aimed only at specific needs and situations. For example, a businessman who travels internationally but typically stays and works in environments where English is spoken might not be interested in achieving native fluency. His goals might be learning how to give basic directions to a taxi driver and acquiring some basic souvenir-shopping lingo. Although he'll still have to learn some basics of the target language, his objectives—and therefore his short-term definition of fluency—are simple, finite, and easily achieved.

Even if you are interested in developing high-level mastery of a language, you'll still have to approach that mastery step-by-step. With a well-structured study plan, you will achieve greater levels of skill in a shorter time than you would by setting higher, less realistic goals. You will also retain a lot more information and be more confident in your abilities by taking a goal-oriented approach.

Rule 4: Communication is always the ultimate goal of applied language study. Understand the importance of context and focus on understanding and being understood.

Another great advantage of establishing lessons based on specific goals or situations is that it gets you used to the

Remember that the ultimate goal in using any language is communication. Make use of body language, your environment, and supplemental tools to amplify your spoken words and get your message across clearly. Here the author's wife uses an electronic calculator—along with an appropriate assortment of frowns, smiles, and head shakes—to break through the language barrier and cut a good deal on some Thai silk.

idea of establishing *context* in your use of a language. Context is defined as "the parts of a discourse that surround a word or passage and can throw light on its meaning." If you know what subject you're talking about, even if you don't understand all the words, you can understand a lot of the meaning through context. Understanding this concept is critical because it is the first step toward grasping the reality of studying another language. That reality is that the ultimate goal of any language study geared toward the practical use of the language is *communication*. Understanding and being understood in the specific situations that are important to you is more important than trying to convince the population of Guangzhou, China, that you, a six-foot-two, blue-eyed blond, are a native speaker of Cantonese.

Rule 5: **Prioritize your goals in a flexible format and be ready to add, remove, or reorganize them to suit the characteristics of your target language. (In other words, when in doubt, lower your standards.)**

If your desire is to achieve a moderate or high level of fluency in your target language, your best bet is to identify a series of goals based on the types of situations you will most likely encounter or the ones that most interest you. Write these goals down on separate note cards or type them into a word processor if you have one. Once you have documented your goals, start prioritizing them based on their level of complexity. Place the easier goals (e.g., learning basic greetings, asking the time) near the top of the pile or list and the more difficult goals (e.g., asking directions, shopping for specific items, debating the long-term political implications of the international arms race) at the bottom.

What you've just done is to prioritize your study of the target language based on *your* goals and interests. That may not seem like much of an accomplishment, but it is really a significant step toward achieving proficiency based on *your personal definition of the term*. And since you are the one we're trying to please, that's a significant step.

The cruel and simple truth is that it takes a hell of a lot of time and work to become completely fluent in another language. Since we're looking at language study as a goal-oriented, situation-specific thing, we can learn what we want when we want (once we have the appropriate basics, of course). If along the way we run into a situation or linguistic need that we hadn't anticipated, we add that scenario to our study list and, if appropriate, shuffle it to the top.

Even if total mastery of a language is your ultimate objective, you'll still have to approach it step-by-step: prioritizing, learning, and ultimately mastering selected portions of the language until your collective knowledge qualifies you as fluent.

Rule 6: All languages are not created equal. Before you study any language, do some research and learn "what" your target language is in terms of its structure and writing system.

If you've already developed a prioritized list of goals for learning your chosen foreign language, the next step is to do a little research on it. If you haven't quite developed your list, this should still be your next step. Without being too redundant, languages *do* differ. And until you develop at least a basic understanding of the nature of your target language, you can't really develop a detailed study plan.

The first step in developing this understanding should be a visit to your local library. There you can peruse a wide variety of books on your chosen language at no cost and do some research into the nature of your target language and the customs and culture of the countries where it is spoken. Although the Internet is also a good source of this kind of overview information, the sooner you get familiar with the different sorts of books available on your language, the better off you'll be.

Getting familiar with the available study materials for your language is critical because it will help you decide in which language you want to study your chosen language. Yes, you read that right. *In many cases, you must decide which language you plan to use to study your target language.* The reason is that not all languages use a romanized (English language–style) alphabet or an easily learned and referenced phonetic alphabet.

To understand this concept, think of a sign printed in Spanish and one printed in Chinese. Even if you don't speak Spanish, you could still use English pronunciation guidelines to approximate the sound of the Spanish words. You wouldn't know what you are saying, but you could do a passable job of faking your way through it phonetically. Not so with the Chinese sign. Each Chinese character has a distinct pronunciation, but its written form provides no phonetic clues to what that is. If you wanted to pronounce the character, you'd have to have the help of a romanization system that uses our alphabet (with some variations) to approximate the Chinese pronunciation. Romanization systems of this type are a convenient way of rendering foreign-language terms with our alphabet and provide a critically important head start to learning those languages. Since some languages have been written or transcribed with more than one romanization system, you'll need to do your homework and choose a standard for your study of the target language.

Rule 7: **In addition to researching your language, research its dialects and try to identify materials that focus on the dialect(s) most relevant to your needs.**

It's also a good idea to find out if there are any major dialects of your target language so you can tailor your studies to your specific needs. For example, Castilian Spanish, spoken in Spain, sounds quite different from Mexican, Puerto Rican, Cuban, and South American Spanish. Although native speakers from these different areas could make themselves understood when out of their native element, you'll get more mileage out of your study by targeting the dialect you'll most likely be using. Again, specific goals make it easier for you to achieve tangible results.

> ¿Qué hay sobre la mesa?
> *Keh I* soh-*breh lah* MEH-*sah?*
> What is on the table?

sa hay un tintero, una caja, unos libros, unos lá
 MEH-*sah I oon teen*-TEH-*roh, oo-nah* KAH-*hah,*
brohs, oo-nohs LAH-*bee-thehs*

พูดได้นิดหน่อยเท่านั้น

เขาพูดภาษาจีนได้ไหม

ได้, ก่อนนี้เขาอยู่ที่ฮ่องกง

ลูกคุณเดวิดเป็นผู้หญิงหรือผู้ช

ผู้หญิง

ลูกเขาพูดภาษาไทยไม่ได้ใช่ไห

One of the most important steps in learning a new language is to research the language itself and find out more about its structure, organization, and special challenges. A good first step is to look at the written form of the language to see what type of alphabet—if any—it uses. Which of these languages do you think would be most difficult to learn?

أنتم عزل !!

ت خطوط امداداتكم ولن يص

نعزيز فلا يهم صدام مصيركم

مصيركم. ألقوا اسلحتكم،

新英汉词典正文 ……………………………………

Rule 8: There is no substitute for quality study materials. Once you know what kind of study materials are available, compare them with your goals and borrow or buy the best materials you can find.

A quality education is the result of quality time spent studying quality materials. Although it's tempting to think that a single pocket phrase book or a couple of audiocassettes are all you need to master your target language, that's not the way it works. If you want to learn a language well, you need to borrow or invest in books, dictionaries, audiocassettes, and other reference materials. If your goals include specialized business or technical situations, you have to invest in specialized reference materials that include the vocabulary and terminology you need.

Unless your language goals are very basic, odds are you will not find one book that will teach you everything you need (or want) to know. Learn to evaluate language materials based on your personal objectives and accept the fact that, in many cases, only a portion of a book or audiocassette may be relevant to those objectives. Buy or borrow what you need when you need it and fill the gaps in your knowledge as you go.

Rule 9: To achieve your personal goals, you need to create a customized language curriculum.

The key to achieving your specific language goals is to have a specific curriculum geared toward those goals. As I've already mentioned, it is unlikely that you will find one book or even one language course that meets all your specific needs. As such, just as you need to invest in a variety of books and language materials, you also have to invest in flashcards, notebooks, and other administrative supplies and use them to create your customized language course. These supplies enable you to draw on your language resources to assemble your own lessons and lesson plan. They also provide a flexible and extremely effective study method that works many times better than simply staring at pages in a book or dozing off listening to an audiocassette.

Your personal language goals will determine whether you'll need a few simple phrase books or an entire foreign language research library. Either way, shop around and buy the best materials you can.

Rule 10: No language is too difficult or too complicated for you to learn. You can do it if you really want to.

Although language study is often viewed as a touchy-feely cultural thing, I'm going to be brutally honest here. If you get frustrated because you can't speak, read, or write as well as you'd like to in your target language, just remember that somewhere out there there's a person who is less educated, less intelligent, and probably less hygienic than you are who speaks that language just fine. Sure, it's his native language. Sure, he's been speaking it all his life. But the bottom line remains: if he can do it, so can you. Redefine your goals as necessary, keep trying, and remember, just as with sex, the only person you have to satisfy is yourself.

Developing a Plan

The next step in your study of a foreign language should be to develop an actual study plan. This plan will allow you to approach your language study in an organized, methodical way that ensures consistent progress. In doing this, you need to remember to be reasonable and to set realistic goals. You also need to be flexible so you can adapt your studies to speed up, slow down, backtrack, or change course to follow new interests and goals.

A truly practical language study program should follow a basic order of events. When learning any skill, it is often said that you must crawl before you can walk and walk before you can run. I guess if we apply this concept to language, you must mumble before you can talk and talk before you can run your mouth. No matter how you look at it, you can't jump ahead too far without learning some basics.

21

If your goal is to learn enough Spanish for a vacation to a popular Mexican tourist area, being able to speak and read a few phrases so that you can order from a menu or hire a taxi may be enough.

In this chapter I give you a guided tour through the process of learning a language effectively. The process I describe is based on my own formal language training in the U.S. military and Department of Defense, advanced university-level language courses, private instruction, and years of living and operating overseas—often in environments where little or no English was spoken. Some of the methods I describe are my own, while others were devised by fellow students, instructors, and some of the best linguists ever employed by our government. The exact process you use may vary slightly depending on the language you are studying and your current proficiency (if any) in other languages.

Please note that some of the steps described here have already been addressed in the previous chapter. If it doesn't make sense to you here, please refer to the earlier sections and make sure you understand the concept thoroughly before you move on.

....

Step 1: Decide on your specific goals and determine how and under what circumstances you will use your language skills.

As explained earlier, your goals will determine your true level of success in studying a foreign language. They will also determine whether you embark on a lifelong study of languages or burn out after a week. No matter how you look at it, you'll be happier learning something you feel is useful than something you consider a waste of time.

So let's set some goals. The way to do this is to first ask yourself *why* you are studying your target language. If you are planning a vacation to a foreign country, what will you be doing there? Will you be hanging out mostly in the tourist areas where some simple phrases and taxi directions are sufficient? Or will you be backpacking across the country in areas populated by very few English speakers? If you plan to shop, what kinds of items are you looking for? What materials are they made of? Are they sold in tourist shops or only in markets that cater primarily to the locals? With whom will you be doing most of your speaking? Waiters and taxi drivers or businessmen and foreign officials? Do you only plan to speak or will you also need to read your target language? If so, what will you be reading, street signs, menus, or legal documents?

Let's say you're not going to travel but want to learn some Spanish to chat with the staff at your favorite Mexican restaurant. Well, if they spoke and understood perfect English, what would you want to say to them? Would you be more interested in discussing their family life and experiences in Mexico or getting the recipe for tortilla soup? Who among the staff would you most like to speak with? The children, whose grasp of English is quite good, or the grandparents of the family who speak little or no English?

Setting realistic goals is about asking yourself honest questions. What you want to do is to break the language down into subsets of vocabulary. By defining a set of circumstances and approaching your study with specific goals

Your personal goals will determine what aspects of a language you choose to study. Many people speak languages like Arabic, Thai, and Chinese reasonably well without ever learning how to read or write them. However, if your goal is to find your way around in an environment like this, reading skill may be a necessity.

based on those circumstances, you can create manageable "lessons." These lessons will enable you to organize your study of a language to suit your personal needs and achieve specific goals in an efficient manner. Over time, they will also allow you to effectively gauge your overall progress in the language and quantify what you've learned.

If you absolutely can't narrow down your goals before you jump in, don't worry about it. Follow some kind of organized program of instruction to get your feet wet and refine your goals as you go.

Step 2: Research your language to become familiar with its overall organization, structure, and writing system.

We discussed this step briefly in the previous chapter, but because I consider it critical to learning a language effectively, I'm going to discuss it in detail here.

Before you begin studying a language, you must have a basic understanding of *what* your target language is and how it is organized. The best way to do this is to talk to someone who has studied the language and achieved a decent level of fluency in it. He or she will know firsthand what challenges the language presents to a nonnative speaker.

If you don't have access to a nonnative speaker, the Internet is a great way of finding brief overviews and descriptions of foreign languages. Your local library will probably also have a variety of resources that will help you get a better idea of the type of language you'll be studying and its similarities to English or any other languages you might have been exposed to previously.

Step 3: Visit your local library and become familiar with the types of materials available on your target language. If you plan on buying language study materials, visit local bookstores, including university bookstores, and see what types of materials are available there and at what cost.

Once you have a basic idea of what your target language is, you'll need to get an idea of what resources are actually available to aid you in your study. For such common languages as Spanish, German, French, and Italian, you should have no problem locating a wide variety of materials. However, if you're intent on learning some obscure African dialect, the odds of finding a comprehensive selection of study materials are not good.

If your target language happens to be an uncommon one, you'll probably have to move up from your local library to a major city library or university library. It is the job of these institutions to find, purchase, and maintain obscure books for the rest of us. Once you know what materials actually exist for your target language, you can see about either getting your own or borrowing the library copies long enough to extract the information you need for your customized curriculum.

Universities and bookstores in college towns can also be a valuable source of used language books and are well worth investigating.

Step 4: **In examining the study materials available to you, pay close attention to the phonetic system used to teach the language. If the writing system of your target language is not a convenient and easily learned phonetic system, the study materials will probably use one or more romanization systems to teach pronunciation. Become familiar with these, try to determine if there is a popular standard, and make the decision to stick with a specific system.**

As I mentioned earlier, all languages are *not* created equal. The ugly truth is that languages that do not have romanized alphabets require a lot more time and effort to learn well. That's just the way it is.

Now before you get all spun up, if your dream is to learn Spanish, Portuguese, French, Italian, German, or any other language that uses an alphabet similar to our English alphabet, you're in good shape. With these languages, you will find it easiest to study the language using its standard written form. If your target language doesn't look very much like English, you may be in for more of a challenge.

A simple test you can use to "size up" the written version of your target language is to find a short passage written in the native language and to try to read it aloud using basic English pronunciation guidelines. It doesn't have to sound good, and you don't need to have any idea what you're saying; you just need to be able to pronounce the words without too much trouble.

If you find that you stumble because you frequently come across letters that don't look like the English alphabet and symbols that make no sense to you, you're probably going to have to invest the extra time to learn the writing system of your target language or use a phonetic system to bridge the gap. If you're learning something like Chinese, which doesn't even *have* an alphabet, a phonetic system is a must.

Time out for a short rant—as I've already mentioned, *no* book can teach you an entire language in 10 minutes a day. Books that promise such miracles are blowing major smoke into an unmentionable area of your anatomy. What's worse is that most of them are based on the idea that English speakers only study foreign languages with romanized alphabets. Many of the tips and tricks they provide therefore only work for languages such as Spanish, French, Italian, etc. Having studied and excelled at such languages as Chinese-Mandarin and Thai, my perspective is a bit different. This book isn't about false promises; it's about helping you to learn better. And sometimes the most important lesson is that the programs that sound too good to be true usually are. Back to the real world. . . .

For languages without alphabets and those that use

alphabets very different from ours, scholars have devised romanization systems. These systems allow English speakers to learn and pronounce the language without having to learn its true alphabet and writing system. Although such romanization systems are convenient and allow you to learn the basics of the language more quickly, they do present a few problems.

The biggest problem has to do with the nature of the scholars who devise them. Scholars thrive on taking credit for things they think up and devote large amounts of their time to disagreeing with other scholars. What this means to the humble language student is that it is quite possible that you will find several different romanization systems for your target language. If it's not challenging enough to learn an entirely different language, try learning it with study materials written in three or four different phonetic systems.

Take a close look at all the materials available on your language and see which ones make the most sense to you. If you notice different romanization systems, spend a few minutes trying to get a feel for each. Also try to find out which system is most prevalent or is used in the materials you find most relevant to your needs. In some cases, there are actually "official" systems of romanization that have been adopted by the countries in which your chosen language is spoken. For example, a number of years ago the People's Republic of China embraced the pinyin system and considers it the one official romanization system for its language. Although that may not be important to you initially, if it affects the type and quality of language materials available to you, it's worth considering. The idea is to standardize your study materials so that all your study efforts use the same romanization system.

Here are two examples of widely used Chinese-Mandarin romanization systems. They both express the same words, but, as you can see, the spellings (and use of a diacritical mark) are very different.

CHINESE CHARACTER ROMANIZATION SYSTEMS

Wade-Giles	Pinyin	English
ch'i	qi	air
pei	bei	north

Step 5: **Identify other unique aspects of your target language and assess the challenges they will present to your learning it.**

Languages, by their very nature, differ significantly. Many foreign languages have characteristics that are critical to their structure and function that simply do not exist in English. Although you should have identified the major quirks of your language back in step 2, now is the time to really get a handle on them. If your target language has one or more of these characteristics, you'll need to program extra time into the early phases of your study schedule to become familiar with them.

For example, Vietnamese, the language at which I am most proficient, is a tonal language. Each syllable of the language has a distinct tone or pitch that helps identify it as a distinct word. Although two words may sound almost alike and be spelled almost alike, if they have different tones, they are in fact different words. All Chinese dialects, Thai, and Lao are also structured this way. Until you wrap your brain around this concept and learn to recognize and produce the different tones, you can't do much with these languages.

On the good side, Vietnamese and most other tonal languages do not conjugate verbs. The verb stays the same whether you're talking about the past, present, or future. Conversely, Spanish, often considered to be an "easy" language, has a conjugation system just as complicated as English, if not more so. As such, you'll spend a lot of your time trying to learn the difference between "I go," "we went," "he will go," "they will have gone," and "don't go there."

Another example is the concept of gender in language. Some languages associate nouns with masculine and feminine genders. For example, in Spanish, "hat" is *el sombrero*—*el* indicating that the noun is masculine. "Life" is *la vida*—*la* indicating a noun that is feminine. To speak these languages well, you need to grasp this concept and apply it properly.

Identifying the unique aspects of your target language is important because people's brains work differently. Some people have no problem with tonal languages but struggle with the ideas of gender and conjugation. Other people's brains work in just the opposite way. They grasp the gender and conjugation stuff but somehow manage to be linguistically tone deaf. Your job is to assess how the specific challenges of your target language will affect your learning curve and structure your study accordingly.

Step 6: **Based on your initial research and your now deeper understanding of your target language, reassess your goals and add, delete, or reprioritize as necessary.**

As I've said before, being realistic is a major key to being successful in your language study. If during research of your target language you identified aspects of the language that might significantly alter your original goals and study plan, it's time to reprioritize. Using the idea of a tonal language again, your original plan might have been to jump right in and start learning how to ask directions and shop for cheap souvenirs. However, once you realize that simply using the wrong tone means the difference between saying "chicken," "train station," and "to run a gambling den," it makes sense to add an entire week of practice just on hearing and pronouncing tones correctly.

Now despite all this talk about identifying your goals and tuning your language study accordingly, I know that some people don't have clear goals in mind and just want to learn another language. Usually, they seek the structure of an organized course and follow along blindly hoping they'll learn what deep down they really want to know. Unfortunately, few organized courses are structured around the way people really speak or want to speak.

If you are one of the folks reading this book because you want to do better in a formal language course taught by an instructor, your organizational work is pretty much done for you. Just look at the table of contents of your textbook and you've got your prioritized list—whether you like it or not. Even though you may not be particularly interested in "Lesson 2: Shopping for Vegetables," you're going to be responsible for it, and you'll need to learn it. However, that doesn't mean that you can't satisfy your personal goals in the process of learning to buy cabbage. If you are in a structured class, learn to make whatever subject you're studying relative to your own personal goals and interests. The basics of shopping are the same whether you're buying vegetables or antiques. If your interest is in antiques, focus on mastering things like numbers, bargaining phrases, adding and subtracting, and the other critical elements of shopping rather than learning how to say "rutabaga" in Japanese. Even when your goals are set for you, you can fine-tune them to achieve what you want out of a language.

You may have noticed that when we first prioritized our goals, we did it using a flexible format—easily rearranged note cards or cut-and-paste elements in a word processor. The reason for this is that languages differ. Because they differ, they must be studied in different ways.

The point of all this is that in addition to *setting* language goals, you must also accept the fact that you will probably be *changing* language goals. As you begin to understand the idiosyncrasies of your target language, you'll identify the skills that you must have to learn it effectively. If those skills do not appear in your list or on any of your goal cards, make a new card and put it in the appropriate place in the stack or type a new goal into your list.

Again, setting practical goals is critical to learning a language. Despite what many other books and so-called experts say, those goals must vary according to the language you choose. By keeping your list of goals flexible, you can adjust your study tactics without losing sight of your objectives.

Step 7: Compare the English content of the various study materials you've found with your goals and select the materials that best represent the types of topics you'd like to focus on.

Books, audiotapes, and videos on language study are expensive, so library research is also a good way to narrow your choices before you invest in language materials of your own. If your goals are very basic, you can probably get by checking out some library materials once or twice and gleaning what you need from them. Although copying such materials may violate copyright laws (and as an author I strongly disapprove of such actions), libraries often have hard-to-find or out-of-print materials that might be specific to your needs. In such cases, a photocopy or bootleg recording might go a long way toward helping your cause. If you're a bit more ambitious, you'll want to invest in quality materials that are relevant to your needs. As with any other job, the better your tools, the better your chances of success.

Once you're up to speed on your target language and the types of study materials available on it in the library, you should repeat the same process at your local bookstores and on the Internet. If you live near a university, pay a visit to its library and bookstore as well. Get a feel for all the different types of study materials available and compare their content with your goals before you decide what's best for you.

The most common types of language study materials you'll find are phrase books, self-study books, textbooks, dictionaries, audiocassettes, video courses, computer programs, and complete multimedia courses. You'll probably also see such things as specialized dictionaries and grammar references. All of these can be useful tools in your study. However, just as it is possible to buy the wrong tool for a job or to have a cheap tool that breaks, you can spend lots of money on materials that don't suit your needs or that teach you exactly what you don't want to know. The following are my general feelings about the various types of study materials and their usefulness.

- **Phrase books.** These are typically pocket-sized references that contain supposedly handy phrases usually expressed in a contrived phonetic system that is supposed to make sense to English speakers. In general, these are of limited use by themselves. When combined with audio- and videocassettes that provide a real guide to pronunciation, they could be useful for a "bare essentials" approach to learning a few useful phrases of a foreign language.

- **Self-study books.** This category consists primarily of the popular books with titles that include the words "instant," "self-taught," and "in 10 minutes a day." The quality and usefulness of these books vary greatly. Some are excellent minicourses that include special pages with adhesive labels, flash cards, and quick-reference guides to common vocabulary and grammar patterns. Others, unfortunately, are superficial, ineffective courses that provide a handful of contrived phrases suitable only for equally contrived situations. These books also often make use of nonstandard phonetic systems to teach pronunciation. Without the aid of a good audio or video pronunciation guide, these books may very well help you invent your own language that only you can pronounce and understand. Shop around for these and review them carefully before you buy.

- **Textbooks.** A good high school freshman text on a foreign language is hard to beat when it comes to comprehensive and reasonably in-depth instruction in a language. These books are often available at a very reasonable cost at used bookstores. Textbooks are great in that they are logically organized and typically present the language in a topical order than makes for easy learning. They also feature lots of exercises to help you practice your skills. On the down side, textbooks are often outdated and focus on archaic speech patterns and on phrases that may not be in common use today. Also, student editions of these texts do not include answers to the questions and drills, leaving you wondering if you really got something right. In general, however, textbooks are a good investment and an excellent model for developing a study plan for your target language.

- **Dictionaries.** Unless you are only interested in learning the bare essentials of a language, sooner or later you'll want to look up a specific word in your target language. To do this you need an appropriate dictionary.

  For most languages there are three basic types of dictionary: (1) native language to target language, (2) target language to native language, and (3) a combination dictionary that includes both. For example, if we assume that since you're reading this you are a native English speaker, you might buy an English-to-Spanish dictionary to look up specific words in Spanish. If you're planning to travel in a Spanish-speaking country and need help reading signs, a Spanish-to-English dictionary might be in order. For convenience, you can kill two birds with one stone and get a dictionary that does both.

  For more complicated languages that do not use romanized alphabets, the plot (and often the dictionary itself) thickens considerably. These languages rarely lend themselves well to combination dictionaries, so you'll probably have to buy one dictionary for each "direction." These languages also cannot be handily organized into alphabetical order, so the method of using the dictionary can be much more involved and time consuming (I've spent an hour looking up one Chinese character!). Once again, you'll have to factor this into your study plan and adjust your goals and study time accordingly.

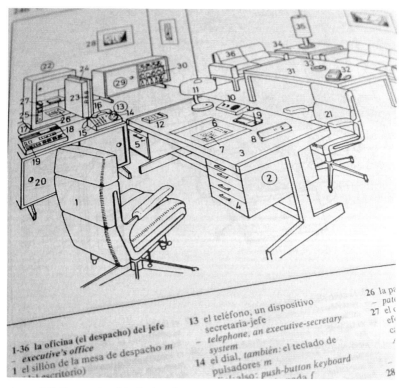

1-36 la oficina (el despacho) del jefe
– executive's office
1 el sillón de la mesa de despacho m
⌐ escritorio)

13 el teléfono, un dispositivo secretaria-jefe
– telephone, an executive-secretary system
14 el dial, también: el teclado de pulsadores m
– also: push-button keyboard

26 la pa
– pat
27 el c
ef
c:
/

28

A good dictionary is critical when learning any foreign language. A selection of good dictionaries is even better. For learning specific situational vocabulary, you can't beat visual dictionaries like this *Oxford-Duden Pictorial Spanish and English Dictionary*.

If you're serious about learning a language, try to get a thick, comprehensive dictionary for both "directions" of your language study. Since language does evolve over time, try to get a recently printed dictionary or revised edition rather than an old one. You should also try to get a smaller but still relatively comprehensive dictionary that you can carry with you when you're out and about.

Finally, if you plan to get into any technical areas of your target language, invest in specialized dictionaries that contain the vocabulary you need. In such circumstances, there is no substitute for technical accuracy. You'll also save precious time that would have been wasted looking for technical terms that simply won't appear in your general-use dictionary. When I was translating documents for official negotiations between the U.S. and Vietnamese governments, I typically used 8 to 10 different dictionaries to ensure that I used the right word to convey the right meaning at the right time.

One excellent resource for both situational and specific technical vocabulary is a pictorial dictionary. These include labeled diagrams arranged by topic and situation and are the best way I've found to get up to speed on topical vocabulary, especially for businessmen.

- **Audiocassettes and CDs.** To speak a language well, you need to model your pronunciation after that of a native speaker. The most convenient way to do this is to buy or borrow a language course that includes prerecorded audiocassettes or CDs. By listening to these materials carefully and mimicking the pronunciation, inflection, and speech patterns they present, you can develop both fluency and a very passable native accent. Because these media are designed for use with portable players, you can also take your language study with you and make good use of otherwise idle time while driving, traveling, or even walking around town.

Note that some so-called quick-study language courses consist only of audio materials, while others pair audio and written materials. The latter is by far the preferred type, since it will allow you to cross-reference the written and spoken forms of the language. Also, no matter how good a speaker may be, there will come a time when you simply cannot hear a word on a tape. By referring to the written materials, you can read the word and reconstruct his statement phonetically.

As with any other language resource, the audio materials you use should be as recent and as relevant to your personal language goals as possible. Although it may be challenging to learn the names of every conceivable tropical fruit in Bulgarian, you'll probably never need that particular linguistic skill.

- **Video courses.** Like audio materials, video courses provide an excellent pronunciation guide after which you can model your speech. However, unlike pure audio materials, language videos also allow you to integrate the visual element of language into your study, drawing additional meaning from body language and physical interaction. As such, they can be an outstanding study resource and a great way to prepare to actually use your language in realistic scenarios.
- **Computer/multimedia courses.** Computer-based language courses are an extremely powerful means of combining audio, video, and written materials into a very dynamic training package. The best software training packages also make language training interactive, providing real-time exercises and quizzes that really test your abilities in the target language. Although more expensive than other

Audiocassettes or CDs are an indispensable part of any language study program because they provide an audio standard after which to model your accent and pronunciation. They can also be used for question/answer practice, comprehension training, and transcription.

types of materials, they can help you achieve your goals more quickly by providing more structure and an increased level of challenge to your language study. Some courses of this type are also targeted to specific language goals (such as business-oriented language study) and may provide a near-turnkey solution to your language study needs.

- **Quick-reference sheets.** These are laminated plastic sheets that provide handy references for commonly used vocabulary and grammar patterns. Most are formatted to fit into a three-ring binder, but depending on your needs and the organization of the sheets, you can sometimes cut them into topic-specific pocket-sized references. Better yet, you can use the templates included in this book to create your own.

- **Internet sources.** There are all kinds of wild things available on the Internet. If you put on your shorts and do a little surfing, you'll find on-line dictionaries, grammar references, translation programs, and more. These can be a great addition to your standard language references and an inexpensive resource for targeted language study. Bear in mind, though, that there is no quality control on the World Wide Web. Just because someone took the time to put up a Web page doesn't mean he took the time to check all the information in that page. Keep a big grain of salt next to your mouse and try to find other ways of corroborating the information you get off the Net.

Step 8: Purchase all the administrative supplies you'll need to support your study efforts and keep them organized.

Once you've obtained your basic language study materials, the next step is to get some office supplies that will allow you to customize your studies to your needs and make studying more convenient and efficient.

The following is a list of materials that I and other experienced linguists have found to be the most useful. Later in the book, I'll describe exactly how to use them to achieve your personal language goals. You'll need the following.

- **Blank flash cards.** These are an effective, inexpensive, and extremely convenient way to learn vocabulary. The best ones are from a company called Vis-Ed, or the Visual Education Association, of Springfield, Ohio. They are 1 1/2 x 3 1/2 inches in size and come in boxes of 1,000. They can be found in office supply stores and college bookstores. If you can't find them, you can use 3-x-5-inch note cards full size or cut into three smaller cards.

- **Cassette recorder, Walkman, and blank audiocassettes.** You want the ability to both listen to and record tapes in your target language. Stick with full-size audiocassettes because they are cheaper and offer longer record times than minicassettes. They are also great if you have a cassette player in your car. A Walkman is great for studying on the run and making use of dead time while waiting for appointments, hanging out in the doctor's office, etc.

- **Post-It notes or removable adhesive labels.** These are great for labeling objects around your house and office with the appropriate nouns in your target language. Labeling is one of the quickest ways of learning the names for common items.

- **A three-ring binder, index tabs, paper, and a matching hole punch.** These materials allow you to create your own textbook for your personal study of a language. Unlike using traditional textbooks and study programs, creating your own allows you to reorder your lessons and add or remove materials based on your needs and interests. This is also better than a typical spiral notebook or journal, which is designed to keep entries in a fixed order. Get in

Labeling your surroundings in your home or office is a great way of surrounding yourself with your target language, keeping your language practice active, and creating direct associations between objects and their foreign-language terms.

the habit of writing language notes in a topic-specific way so that you can insert your notes into the appropriate sections of your binder. Some of the basic topic headings you'll want to start with include grammar notes, idiomatic expressions, vocabulary, specialized vocabulary, body language notes, cultural notes, etc.

- **VCR, DVD player, television, blank video cassettes, and TV guide.** Check your local TV listings to see if you can find any television programs in your target language. If so, you want to record some of the more useful ones and use them as study resources. The VCR and TV can also be used to view prerecorded video courses on your target language and movies and videos in that

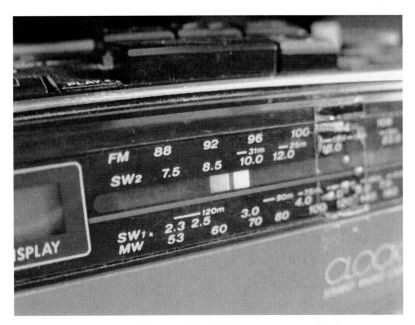

A shortwave radio, especially one with a built-in cassette recorder, is a great way to gain access to foreign-language radio broadcasts. Internet radio sites are also a great source for such broadcasts, which will challenge your comprehension of your target language.

language that you get from your local library or purchase commercially.

If you are really motivated and either travel to a country where your language is spoken or know someone who lives there, you might be able to purchase videos in your target language or record local television broadcasts there for later study.

- **Shortwave radio and cassette recorder.** When I was studying Vietnamese, I used to listen to Voice of America news broadcasts on a shortwave radio to practice my comprehension and learn the vocabulary for current events. For comparison, I also listened to Vietnamese national radio for a more socialist look at the same issues. My shortwave radio had a built-in cassette recorder that allowed me to record and replay the broadcasts to analyze them in greater detail.

With the benefit of the Internet, you can tap into much of this same programming and spare yourself all the tuning and antenna twisting I had to suffer through.

- **Computer and word processor.** If you have a computer, you're well on your way to the Internet access I mentioned previously. If not, head back to the public library and enjoy the benefits of your tax dollars by using their computers. The greatest benefits of computing on your own are (1) you can organize and format your notes much more easily with a word processor; (2) many word processors, such as Microsoft Word, include text sets for foreign languages; and (3) you can study computer-based language courses in the comfort of your own home.

Step 9: Learn the phonetic system of your target language and, if necessary, an associated romanization system.

Now it's time to actually start learning your language. The first step in doing so is to get familiar with the way it sounds. Basic courses that include audio- or videocassettes are great for this, since they typically begin with a lesson in phonetics. Pay close attention to this section and don't hurry through it. Take the time to do the various exercises and make an honest effort to say the sounds out loud in your normal speaking voice. Don't whisper, mumble, or just mouth the words—speak. By getting used to actually producing the component sounds of your target language, you are training yourself and developing the confidence to speak it for real.

When learning the sounds of your new language, pay attention to unusual sounds that don't have a direct English equivalent. Use any hints your materials provide to form your mouth correctly and try to identify English words or combinations of English words that will help you "cross-

Would you know that this was the hotel you were looking for in Luxor, Egypt, if the address was in Arabic only?

train" into your target language. For example, many Asian languages have initial "ng" sounds—a consonant cluster that occurs in English but never at the beginning of a word. To learn this unusual sound more easily, say a word that ends in "ng" and follow it immediately with your new word. For example, the Cantonese word for "I" is *ngóh*. To practice saying this, you might tack it on to the end of the word "sing," forming s*ingóh*. As you get familiar with this hybrid word, start de-emphasizing the "si" sound and emphasizing the *ngóh*. After a while, you'll be a lot more comfortable with producing the initial "ng" sound.

ຂອຍ	ໝາກແຕງ	ນຳເຈົ້າ	ຫຼາຍໜ່ວຍ
	ໝາກເລັ້ນ		ກິໂລ
	ຜັກບົ່ວ		ມັດ
	ນ້ຳອົບອິກ		ຫຼາຍຢ່າງ
	ຢາ ອິກ		ຫຼາຍຢ່າງ

kohy⁶ seu⁵	mak⁶ dtaeng¹	na:m³ chao:⁵	lai⁴ nuay²
	mak⁶ le:n²		gi' lo³
	pa:k³ bua²		ma:t²
	na:m⁵ o:p³ ik⁶		lai⁴ yang²
	ya' ik⁶		

I buy	cucumbers	from you	many pieces.
	tomatoes		kilo.
	onions		bundle.
	more perfume		many things.
	more medicine		

— 6 3 —

To learn a language that does not use a romanized alphabet, like Lao, you will probably have to find study materials that include some form of romanized phonetic system. Here the same sentence is shown in Lao (top), romanized phonetic Lao (middle), and English (bottom). The numbers in the phonetic version indicate the appropriate tone for each syllable. Tones are voice inflections that are an integral part of the word itself and a considerable challenge for a foreigner trying to learn the language.

As you're getting used to the sounds of your new language, you should also try relating those sounds to some kind of written language. If your target language uses a phonetic writing system, you're in luck in that you have a written form that corresponds exactly to the sounds of the spoken form. That's good. However, if you're studying Russian, for example, you'll find that its Cyrillic alphabet, although phonetic, requires dedicated study to learn not only the symbols but also the sounds associated with them. Languages like Thai, Korean, Japanese, Hebrew, and Arabic also have alphabets, but they don't look anything at all like English letters and take a lot of time and diligent effort to learn.

If you don't have the time to learn the true writing system of your target language or if doing so is inconsistent with your goals, you'll need to find study materials that provide a romanized phonetic reference. In some cases (e.g., Chinese pinyin) these systems have been officially adopted and used in many different types of books and references. This is a plus because it allows you to cross-reference and draw what you need from various sources.

In other cases, the phonetic systems represent the authors' ideas of how to simulate foreign-language pronunciation using the English alphabet. Since different authors often have different ideas, your phonetic reference for your target language can easily end up like half-eaten alphabet soup.

If your chosen language has a standardized, romanized phonetic system, take the time to learn it well. If that language doesn't, pick out the best books you can find on the language and compare the systems they use. Then choose one and figure out how to cross-reference the others to it so you can establish it as *your* standard. This is important because you will need to translate words you learn from other sources to your standard phonetic system and to transcribe (write down phonetically) new words that you learn from television, conversations, and other sources.

One final word on romanization systems: if you're not a seasoned linguist, avoid the temptation to make up your own. Unless your target language has phonetic patterns very similar to English and your linguistic goals are very basic, you'll soon find that the phonetic system you conjured up gets confusing, inconsistent, and everything *but* systematic.

Step 10: Identify characteristics and nuances of your target language that are critical to its structure and use and get these concepts clear in your head.

Seasoned linguists often refer to a turning point in their language study when they actually started *thinking* in a foreign language. What this means is that they reached a point where their logical process of formulating and expressing sentences paralleled the linguistic structure of the foreign language. Rather than composing an entire thought in English and then trying to transform that thought into the target language, their minds began assembling the thoughts using the component parts of the foreign language. Moreover, they assembled these thoughts using the order, rules, and logic of that language.

By developing a thorough understanding of the characteristics and quirks of your target language first, your study of the language can be based on an acceptance of them rather than a contrived word-for-word transformation of English. For example, many European languages are structured around the concept of gender, assigning masculine, feminine, and neuter genders to all nouns. You need to develop a thorough understanding of this concept early in your study so it becomes part of your foundation of knowledge of that language. Every time you learn a new noun, make the gender classifier an integral part of that learning process. Since it is functionally an inseparable part of the noun, accept that fact and structure all your study and practice to integrate those elements.

Similarly, the basic grammatical structure of your target language will tell a lot about the logic behind it. Some languages do not follow English's standard "subject + verb + object" formula and place the verb at the end of the sentence. Adjectives modifying nouns may also appear in a specific place, either before or after the noun being modified. By looking at the literal translation of the standard sentence structures of your target language, you will often get a good insight into the logic and thought process behind the language. Once again, you must accept this and try to use it as a foundation for your ability to think in the foreign language.

The sooner you accept and grasp the core elements of your target language, the better your chances of developing usable skills in that language. These elements simply become a "given," freeing you to explore the more creative and expressive aspects of your language goals.

Step 11: Using your personalized, prioritized list of goals and objectives, begin your study of the language.

This is how you learn the language on your terms. Using the resources you've compiled, find the lessons and vocabulary that are most relevant to your primary goals. If a particular book or resource provides a ready-made lesson for your needs, use it as a foundation and build on it with vocabulary and phrases from other sources.

Don't be afraid to skip ahead in a particular book to get the information you need. Again, you're out to satisfy your goals. However, if you realize that Chapter 7, "Ordering Food in a Restaurant," refers to grammar patterns and concepts in previous chapters, backtrack as necessary to fill in the gaps.

One of the most useful, and therefore common, approaches to learning the use of a language is the concept of replacement. Replacement exercises typically begin with a simple statement using a particular grammar pattern. After repeating the initial statement a few times, you are prompted to replace the noun in the sentence with a different noun from the vocabulary list. In the next exercise, you may keep the noun the same and replace the verb. Later you may be challenged to replace both.

Use this concept to adapt lessons that topically are not of great interest to you but contain useful grammar patterns and phrases to your personal needs and goals. For example, you may not be interested in a chapter based on buying flowers at the market. No problem. Highlight and extract the core elements of the chapter—phrases and grammar patterns related to buying, selling, paying, and getting change—and use them as the basis for your own lesson. Replace petunias and chrysanthemums with the kinds of stuff you might really want to buy and build a lesson to suit your own needs and interests.

Step 12: After a few study sessions, and after gaining a deeper understanding of your target language, reassess your goals and adjust accordingly.

As you begin to make some progress in your studies, go back and reexamine your goals. If you realize that you set the bar a little too high initially, adjust your priorities and make sure that you have enough basic elements to provide a foundation for achieving your higher goals. By organizing your study materials in a flexible way, you will be able to easily customize your curriculum to meet your needs.

You'll also want to take a hard look at your study schedule and come up with something reasonable that allows you to devote adequate time to be productive without bringing the rest of your life to a screeching halt. For best results, try to budget a reasonable block of time (preferably at least 30 minutes) at least three days a week to work on your language. This will give you enough time to actually accomplish something and will ensure that you do it frequently enough to avoid forgetting too much information between sessions.

An even better way of establishing a language study schedule is to identify periods of idle or underused time and figure out how to work your language study into those windows of opportunity. One of the best ways to do this is by making use of your commuting time to and from work. Rather than spending your time listening to the radio or cursing at other drivers, use it to listen to language tapes and work on your comprehension and pronunciation. Equip your car with a cassette or CD player and listen to either commercial or homemade audio lessons containing vocabulary lists, quizzes, and comprehension exercises. You can also use this time to talk to yourself, practicing your pronunciation out loud to polish your speaking ability.

By taking a good, objective look at your goals, your schedule, and your real level of motivation, you will be able to tune your foreign language study program to suit your true needs and interests. You won't become fluent in a week, but you'll also be less likely to become frustrated and quit after a week. Restructure your goals and study to keep the program interesting and to allow you to always make progress in your study. If you do this, you will be much more likely to achieve your language goals.

Strategies and Tips for Optimizing Your Language Study

In this section of the book I present 50 of my favorite language study tips and strategies. Most of these are methods that I have developed or used myself, but they also include tips that I have culled from professional linguists at the U.S. State Department, NSA, CIA, DIA, and other U.S. and foreign government agencies. Others come from some of the most accomplished yet least recognized linguists in the world: merchants who make their living trading across cultures and language barriers.

These strategies have been proven to produce better learning results in less time than traditional study methods. While they are all potentially effective, bear in mind that different people learn in different ways, therefore some methods may be better suited to your needs than others.

Become familiar with all the methods listed here and experiment with the ones that seem best suited for your needs. Try them first as they are described here; then, based on your own first-hand experience and needs, feel free to modify them as necessary to achieve the best results.

Note that I have organized these methods based on the types of skills they develop and the types of applications they best support. This will further aid you in choosing the strategies that are most appropriate for your personal linguistic goals.

GENERAL STUDY STRATEGIES

Tip 1. **Try to grasp the literal meaning of the speech patterns in your target language so you can learn to "think" in that language.**

One of the most common mistakes people make when trying to learn and use a foreign language is translating an English idea word for word into the target language. In some cases this works, but in many others it sounds incredibly stupid. For example, "good morning" translated word for word into Spanish yields *"buenos días,"* which is perfectly correct. However, the same approach does not work at all in Chinese-Mandarin, which uses the morning greeting *"zao,"* which simply means "early."

All languages are a reflection of the cultures that created them. As such, they reflect the logic, ideas, and concerns that are prevalent in that culture. Your goal as an aspiring linguist must therefore be to understand how native speakers of your target language think and how they express those thoughts and ideas in words. The ability to do this directly, without an intermediate English step, is the mark of a true linguist. In other words, you understand a situation based on the actual conditions, circumstances, or needs that exist, and then you express the appropriate thoughts in your target language. You do *not* see the situation, formulate thoughts in English, and then try to transform those thoughts into a foreign language.

Learning about the culture of the countries where your target language is spoken will give you a deeper understanding of the language and the logic behind it. Here the author (far right) performs a song in Vietnamese with other nonnative speakers at a Tet (Vietnamese Lunar New Year) celebration in Bangkok.

For example, when you see a person for the first time in the morning, common courtesy dictates that you should greet him. Rather than thinking in English that you must say "good morning," simply think of the requirement to offer the appropriate greeting in your target language and do it.

This approach allows you to relate the reality of a situation directly to your target language and is the real key to developing fluency in any language.

Tip 2.   Use cognates as shortcuts to fluency.

Cognates are words that are very similar in nature, usually because they share the same linguistic origin. For

The English word *police* and the Spanish word *policia* are cognates. They both come from the French word *policier*. Cognates can make learning a foreign language much easier.

example, the Spanish word *computadora* looks and sounds very much like its English equivalent "computer." Obviously, this makes learning and remembering the Spanish word much easier because you can relate it to an English meaning that is already very familiar to you.

One way to accelerate your study of a language is to become familiar with its cognates and use them to help form a foundation for your vocabulary. Cognates can include all different parts of speech, so don't forget to look for familiar-sounding verbs, adverbs, adjectives, pronouns, and other parts of speech.

If your goals include the study of more than one language, especially languages in the same linguistic family, you'll find cognates a very important part of your learning method. It is easier to learn Italian if you already know how to speak Spanish because they share many words that qualify as cognates. Similarly, when I learned Vietnamese after having studied Chinese-Mandarin, I was able to learn and recall many Vietnamese vocabulary words much more readily because of their similarity to the comparable Chinese words.

One word of caution: although many like-sounding words can be useful cognates, there are also many false cognates—words that look and sound alike but mean very different things. So be careful. When cognates work for you, be grateful and use them to your advantage. When they don't, make sure you can separate similar words and keep their meanings straight in your head.

Tip 3.   Use flash cards as a convenient, portable, and flexible means of learning and testing yourself.

Despite their simplicity, flash cards are probably the most effective means of learning foreign language vocabulary ever developed. Whether you purchase them precut or make your own from index cards, these simple devices are much more effective than learning vocabulary words from a page format or list.

First of all, the act of preparing flash cards forces you to write all the target words and their meanings down—an action that starts the process of internalizing the words and their meanings. Once the cards are finished, your first study phase should be to read the foreign language word aloud and then turn the card over to reveal its English meaning. After doing this several times to the entire stack of cards, flip the stack over. Now start with the English meaning and see if you can produce the proper foreign language response. If you get one wrong, place that card in a separate stack. When you've worked your way through all the words, pick up the stack of words you got

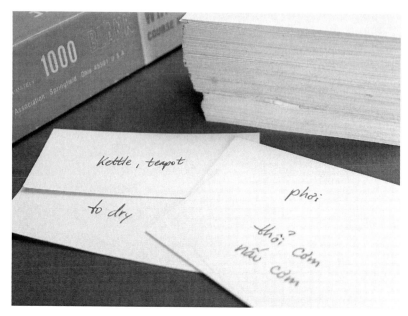

Flash cards are an inexpensive yet highly effective means of learning foreign language vocabulary. You can also take them with you wherever you go and turn otherwise idle time into study time.

wrong and focus on it, again creating a pile for correct answers and one for incorrect answers.

By studying in this way, you can easily separate the words that give you the most trouble and focus on them until you get them right.

If you are studying a language that conjugates verbs, don't just make flash cards for the infinitive form of the verbs. Take the time to make separate cards for all the different persons and tenses. This will allow you to study and produce these spontaneously and directly rather than trying to mechanically conjugate a verb in the middle of a sentence.

Tip 4. **Use picture flash cards to allow you to associate objects and actions directly with the appropriate words in the target language.**

In addition to text-based flash cards, make flash cards that consist of a picture of an object or action on one side and the target language term for it on the other side. Once again, this prompts you to relate things directly to the target language rather than passing through an intermediate English-language step and gives you a huge head start toward fluency.

This method is often used to teach toddlers how to speak. Flash cards for children typically consist of a picture of an object on one side and the English word for that object on the other. If you can find flash cards like this in your native language, buy them and use them. If not, or if the children's flash cards don't cover everything you want to learn, make your own by shooting photos, clipping pictures from magazines, or drawing sketches for the picture side of the flash cards.

Tip 5.   Use audiocassettes and CDs as a model for your pronunciation, as well as a test of your accent.

Learning a language is half "breaking the code" and half learning to mimic other people's speech. Although mimicry alone will not make you fluent, it is a very important part of developing a good accent and near-native pronunciation. In my experience, the ability to pronounce a limited vocabulary well and be understood immediately is more effective than knowing a large number of words and phrases and pronouncing them all poorly.

When studying any foreign language, you should listen and mimic a lot. Don't be lazy in your practice. Instead, really try to emphasize the proper pronunciation and tone of your target language. In fact, you might even want to overemphasize them to really become comfortable with the vocal characteristics of the language. As you get better and start speaking a bit more quickly, you can back off on your accent to achieve a relaxed yet accurate native-sounding pronunciation.

Although this process may seem a bit dramatic at first,

it is really the only way to cultivate a good accent, which, by the way, is a significant part of fluency in a language.

When I was studying Vietnamese, I had a young female army private in my class from Tennessee. Although she was reasonably bright and understood the material presented, she spoke Vietnamese with the same slow, drawling country twang with which she spoke English. Even though her spoken sentences were grammatically correct, they never sounded quite right and were typically difficult to understand. Fortunately, for the army and Vietnamese speakers everywhere, she got pregnant, married, and out of military service.

If you're still not convinced that an authentic accent is worth the effort, think of the worst nonnative English accent you've ever heard and put yourself in that person's shoes. Just as you may have laughed at him, native speakers of your target language will laugh at you. Don't give them that chance. Work hard to develop a good accent.

After listening to your audiotapes for a while and repeating the words and sentences they present, test your pronunciation by recording yourself speaking the same words. Then play the recorded tape back and compare your accent to that of the native speaker on the source tape. Give your accent an honest critique and use your recorded tape to identify aspects of your pronunciation that need improvement.

Once your pronunciation is reasonably clear and accurate, begin recording your own tapes to suit the needs of your customized curriculum. You can use these tapes to present new vocabulary, to quiz yourself, to ask yourself questions, and even to present one-half of a situational conversation. Make several tapes like this and then put them away for a week or two before you listen to them. When you go back to them, they will seem fresh and will prompt you to provide spontaneous responses. When you get to the point where you know a tape too well, make a new one and shelve the other one for a few months before you go back to it for review.

Although cassette tapes are by far the most convenient means of audio learning, if you have a computer and the proper software, you can also burn your own audio CDs to achieve the same goals.

Tip 6. **Don't always practice your listening compre-hension in a quiet environment. Introduce ambi-ent noise in your listening practice so you can learn to deal with it in the real world.**

At first, you'll want to listen to your language tapes in a quiet environment that allows you to concentrate and hear every word clearly. Like anything else, you must learn to walk before you can run. Real conversations, however, rarely occur in pristine, quiet environments. When you use a language for real, you may be standing on a busy street corner, in a crowded restaurant, or in the middle of a bustling market. Wherever you may be, you won't have the luxury of asking everyone (including the goats and pigs) to be quiet while you try to figure out what's being said.

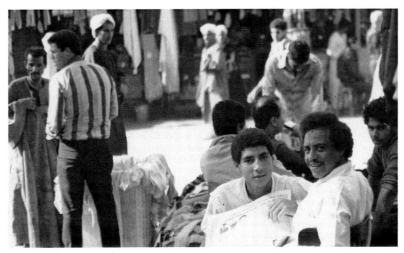

When you try converse in the real world, you probably won't have the luxury of a quiet environment. Make sure you practice under conditions that simulate lifelike conditions, such as this bustling market in Aswan, Egypt.

When I was training to be an electronic warfare/signals intelligence voice intercept operator (military speak for someone who eavesdrops on foreign radio communications), we typically spent two to three hours a day listening to language tapes in a lab. Initially, these tapes were very clear, featuring well-modulated voices talking away at a leisurely pace. As time went on, however, the tapes began to simulate the reality of actual military radio communications, including rapid, slurred speech, fading and intermittent signals, and two or more speakers talking simultaneously. By the end of the one-year course, the audio quality of the tapes we listened to was horrendous and included everything from diesel engine noise to interference from signals in other languages to gunfire. Despite the challenges all this ambient noise provided, we were still able to hear and understand what was going on—because we trained for it. If you plan to use your language in the real world, you need to train for it as well.

One of the best ways to learn to deal with ambient noise is to use a Walkman or other portable tape player equipped with cheap, over-the-ear headphones. Don't get the expensive ones that exclude outside noise or fit snugly into your ears; get the kind with the round foam pads about the size of your earlobes. Now, load up your language tape and go somewhere noisy—a bench on a busy street corner, a cafeteria, a bowling alley—anywhere. Don't turn the volume up too loud, but let the ambient noise filter through. This effectively simulates the way your target language will sound in the real world. At first you'll feel frustrated. With practice, however, you'll learn to filter out the junk and focus on the content of the tape.

Initially you'll want to do this with your standard practice tapes. As you get better, repeat the same drill with tapes recorded from foreign-language radio and television broadcasts and tapes you make yourself to really test your comprehension under realistic conditions.

Tip 7. **If you know native speakers of your target language, ask them to make practice tapes for you that are specifically geared toward your linguistic goals.**

As previously noted, audiotapes featuring the voices of native speakers are your best source of authentic models for your accent and the best way of learning to understand real spoken foreign language. However, since you are interested in developing a customized curriculum to suit your personal linguistic goals, it may be difficult to find tapes that adequately address the things you want to learn. The answer to this problem is to have a native speaker (or at least a speaker with near-native fluency) record custom audiotapes for you.

Finding someone to make language study tapes for you depends largely on your target language and your networking skills. If you are in a formal language class, talk to the teacher and ask him if he'd be willing to record a few tapes for you. If necessary, offer to pay him for his time.

If you are not in a formal class, talk to your friends, visit restaurants, contact local universities, or do whatever other networking is necessary to locate a fluent speaker of your target language. Ideally, you want to find one who also speaks English well and can understand your language goals. Describe the types of situations you'd like to prepare for and make up a list of phrases, questions, and vocabulary that you'd like included in your custom audiotape. Ideally, you want to leave blank spaces next to each item on the list so either you or your native speaker can fill in the written form for each. Once you've organized your lesson, discuss it with your speaker and record your tape. Again, you may want to pay him a nominal fee or compensate him in some way for his time and effort. If he is still studying English, you might be able to arrange an even trade and make custom study tapes for him.

Note that for the sake of convenience I am using primarily masculine references in this book. Obviously, it is also a good idea to obtain audiotapes featuring female speakers so that you can become familiar with hearing your foreign language spoken with a female voice. Since the spoken form of some languages, such as Thai, is slightly different for males and females, finding a female speaker could be very important to your study efforts. Again, researching the nature and characteristics of your target language is the key to identifying such nuances.

Tip 8. If you have the opportunity to use your target language with a native speaker, record it if possible.
Pocket-sized microcassette or digital recorders are an excellent investment for the aspiring linguist. In addition to adapting their traditional use—making verbal notes to yourself—to your language study goals, you can use them to record your conversations with other speakers of your target language. Whether the conversation is planned in advance or completely spontaneous, you should first ask the other person's permission to record it before you whip out your recorder. Explain that you are trying to improve your abilities in your target language and consider your conversation an excellent learning opportunity.

After you've successfully recorded a conversation, replay the tape and try to cull as much information from it as possible. Have a dictionary handy so you can look up any words that you didn't recognize the first time around. Take note of the native speaker's speech patterns, grammar, terms of address, and any colloquial phrases he might have used and add these to your notes and flash cards as appropriate. Listen carefully to his accent and compare it with your own, looking for ways of improving your pronunciation and inflection to make it more authentic.

If you are like most people, as you replay the conversation, you will naturally "Monday-morning quarterback" your responses and kick yourself for not saying all the things you knew but couldn't bring to the surface at the time of the conversation. Rather than just kicking yourself, use this as a learning opportunity and a second chance. Play a portion of the native speaker's side of the conversation and then pause the tape and say your new, improved response or a different response altogether. In this way you can get a lot of linguistic "mileage" out of a single conversation.

Tip 9. Talk to yourself (preferably when no one else is around).

Every new speaker of a foreign language is self-conscious when speaking in front of others. Despite this fact, few students make the effort to speak out loud when they are *not* in front of others. This is your chance to say whatever you want, as many times as you want, without fear of embarrassment.

Talking to yourself can take many forms depending on your personal study goals. If you are trying to develop general conversational skills, you can practice describing what's going on around you, outlining the events of your day, explaining a process to someone, or asking questions about someone's background, etc. You can even play one or more roles in a conversation to practice both questions and answers.

Another great way of practicing your language is to simply describe verbally to yourself some of your routine daily activities. Practice describing your actions while you cook dinner, clean the house, do laundry, or anything else. The idea is to make using the language as natural as the actions you are describing and to put you in touch with the vocabulary and sentence structure associated with everyday objects and actions.

Like any other skill, the only way to get better at speaking a language is to actually practice speaking. Although thinking, whispering, and mumbling can help to a degree, they work best only if your goal is to think about, whisper, or mumble your target language. If you want to learn to speak, speak!

Tip 10. Accept your chosen language as it is. Don't try to change it to fit you, because you're outnumbered.

As simple and basic as this might sound, this concept is still lost on many beginning and even advanced language students. As I mentioned elsewhere in this book, every language is a direct reflection of the cultures that created it. Just as you as an individual are pretty much powerless to change the culture of an entire country, you aren't going to convince any native speakers of your target language to change their speech patterns to match yours. They also don't owe you any explanations for the way they do things.

When I was studying Chinese-Mandarin at the DLI back in 1980, I had a U.S. Navy enlisted classmate who insisted on asking why certain aspects of Chinese were the way they were. Each time we learned a new nuance of Chinese—like the fact that it doesn't use verb conjugation but indicates tenses with particles—this guy would raise his hand and ask the instructor why it was done that way. After hearing this pointless question asked numerous times, the instructor, a rather stern fellow named Mr. Bai, finally blurted out, "It's the Chinese way!" Well, he was right. It *is* the Chinese way, and there wasn't—and still isn't—anything we can do about it, except to learn it their way.

So how does all this help *you* learn *your* target language? It does so in two ways. First, it should dissuade you from asking why your language is different because you now know that asking such a thing is a waste of time. This will allow you to concentrate on learning. Second, it should discourage you from lowering your standards and speaking your foreign language as a bastardized foreign-English mix that nobody but you understands.

The bottom line is that if you are going to learn a foreign language, you have to learn it according to its own standard. The good news is that you still get to use our methods so you can get there a bit sooner.

Tip 11. Use onomatopoeia to learn and remember words in your target language.

Onomatopoeia refers to words that sound like the meanings—usually actions—that they represent. Several good English examples include "buzz," "hiss," and "swoosh."

Many foreign languages, particularly Asian languages, are very descriptive in nature and use onomatopoeia a lot. Unlike English words, which are often based on the roots of other languages, their vocabularies are more pure and direct. In many cases, the word for something is simply a vocal imitation of the sound of that action or thing.

Onomatopoeia is a great way of learning and remembering foreign vocabulary because it provides very distinct hints. Whether you are trying to recall the meaning of a foreign word or trying to recall the pronunciation of that word to use it in a sentence, the vocal clues onomatopoeia provides can be very helpful.

Tip 12. Learn to listen before you talk.

Many beginning linguists are obsessed with speaking—even when they don't know how to say anything. As noted elsewhere, you do need to speak to become truly proficient at your language; however, the best way to have something to say is to base it on what someone else said.

We all know that children learn to speak by mimicking adults. That's just the way language works. Well, given this fact, consider yourself—the adult wannabe foreign-language speaker—a child in the foreign country where your language is spoken. Better yet, since you're older and a little more worldly than the average two-year-old, you're the equivalent of an exceptionally intelligent child. When it comes time to learn how to talk, you have two choices: you can babble in English or some bastardized half-foreign language (the equivalent of unintelligible baby talk to the adults around you), or you can shut up and listen until you're ready to try imitating the adults by speaking their language. That's how kids learn language and how they ultimately get what they want. It's also the best way to get what you want out of your foreign language study.

Another important reason to learn to listen first is that in many cases your objective in using a foreign language is to get information from someone who speaks that language. For example, if you want to learn how to ask for directions, you'll need to understand the answer you get. As such, listening becomes a critically important skill.

The first nine years of my intelligence career were focused on listening, or collection as it was called. My job was to listen to people speaking and figure out both what they were saying and whether that information was of value or not. Throughout this entire process, they never knew I was listening and I never had the opportunity to ask questions. I simply took what I heard and made the best sense of it I could.

When I finally started working in the HUMINT (human intelligence) field and had the opportunity to actually talk to people, I found that my listening skills paid big dividends. Not only did I understand what was being said, I was able to draw out additional details through follow-up questions and body language, and by comparing the interviewee's story with other intelligence information. Since I wasn't struggling to understand what was being said, I had a lot more time and energy to manipulate the interview and play small-scale Cold War politics—a challenging but tremendously enjoyable subset of language use.

Tip 13.   Master numbers in your target language.

When studying to be a voice intercept operator, I was tested on number recognition every day. At first, it was simple—single digits, double digits, and a few numbers in the hundreds. After a while, we got into the thousands, ten thousands, hundred thousands, and millions. By the time we were six months into the course, our daily number tests consisted of 50 number sequences, each consisting of about five random groups of four to six digits each, or an average

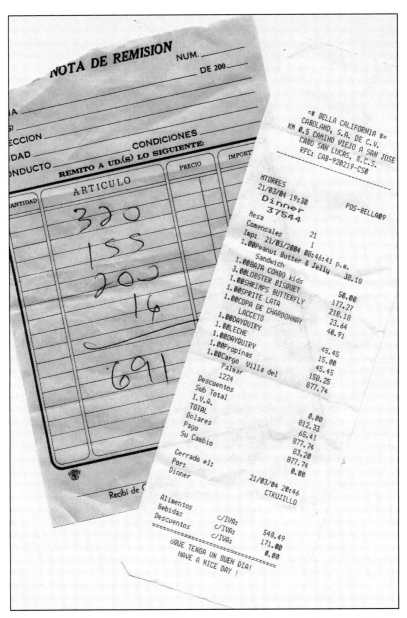

Mastering numbers in your target language will make everything simpler from shopping to renting a vehicle to making a phone call.

of about 30 numbers per sequence. Fifty sequences of roughly 30 numbers each is 1,500 numbers, all read in a single pass (no repeats) in about eight minutes.

As with all our tests, if you couldn't hack numbers, you didn't pass and you became a member of DLI's 60 percent attrition rate. If you could hack the number tests, you never had a problem understanding numbers again. It became second nature—just like your hearing and understanding a number in English.

If you think about it, numbers occur everywhere in language. You'll hear and use them in prices, addresses, phone numbers, and countless other contexts (pun intended). As such, you need to make them second nature. Practice numbers a lot, both as individual digits and as large numbers at least in the hundreds, thousands, and ten thousands. If your language is related to cultures that have a particularly poor exchange rate (meaning you'll get big fat stacks of their money every time in exchange for a few U.S. dollars), you may want to spend some time on even larger numbers, in the hundred thousands and millions. When you're on the ground in a foreign country and the numbers start flying, you'll be glad you did.

Tip 14. Learn about the terms of address in your target language and figure out how to keep yours simple and polite.

Many foreign languages base their terms of address on the members of the typical family unit. Rather than "me," "you," "he," and "they," their terms of address are more like "brother," "sister," "grandpa," and "uncles." Needless to say, the learning curve for this seemingly simple aspect of a language can become pretty steep.

Other languages do not go to this extreme but choose to distinguish between formal or polite terms of address and familiar (and sometimes even vulgar) terms of address. The term you choose becomes an instant and very obvious statement of your respect (or lack thereof) for the person you are addressing. Get it right and you're a skilled linguist with exceptional insight into the foreign culture. Get it wrong and you just called a high-ranking government official "dude."

If your linguistic goals are relatively simple or if you're still in the early stages of learning and using your language, your best bet is to stick with simple, respectful terms that will allow you to cover most of your personal pronoun bases without too much brain cramp. Although this may mean calling everyone from a five-year-old boy to a 95-year-old great-grandfather "sir," the chances of offending someone are pretty slim.

Some languages also have generic, polite terms that can be used in place of personal pronouns. If your language is one of these, take the easy way out until you can master the more complicated terms of address.

As far as vulgar terms of address go, they rarely have a place in casual conversation and can usually be ignored. However, in rare circumstances they can be used with great effect. Once, while working in Vietnam, a group of local hoods took exception to my team's presence in "their" restaurant. Having faced a drunken Vietnamese official threatening me with an AK-47 just the day before, I was in no mood for games. When the taunts of the hoods finally reached a fever pitch, I stood up and confronted them with carefully chosen terms of address and curse words that would have made a Vietnamese sailor proud. As I did, I also opened the Filipino butterfly knife I was carrying with a great flourish and buried it into the table in front of me. Although I'm sure it was my linguistic skill that broke their spirit, the knife trick didn't hurt. Either way, they quickly left with their tails tucked between their legs.

Tip 15. Learn to ask questions in the form of "statement + is that correct?"

One great way to rack up a lot of speaking practice while reinforcing proper sentence structure is to make a habit of repeating and confirming what a native speaker tells you. For example, if someone is giving you directions and tells you to go straight for two blocks and then turn left, you'd say, "I go straight for two blocks and then turn left, is that correct?" Just like a cassette tape, this tactic allows you to model your speech after that of a native speaker immediately after he completes his statement. It also teaches you a useful trick that works well with most languages.

Simple questions using simple interrogatives are usually not too challenging for beginning linguists. However, once the idea behind your question starts getting more complicated, you have to work a lot harder to phrase the question properly. One easy way around this is to explain the idea as a statement and then turn it into a question by adding a phrase like "is that correct?" or "isn't that so?" This concept exists formally in Spanish, where any statement can be transformed into a question by adding ¿verdad? to the end. Other languages share the same concept, but even if your target language doesn't, you can still get the idea across by using a statement and a simple question back to back.

Tip 16. Avoid complex conjugation by learning to use auxiliary, or helping, verbs.

One of the greatest challenges of learning a language is learning how to conjugate verbs. To speak well, you need to be able to accurately modify verbs to correspond to the proper personal pronoun and correct tense of the verb. If you can't do this well, you end up saying things like "Yesterday they is here."

Although you can use the flash-card strategies mentioned earlier to accelerate your learning of verb conjugation, if your linguistic goals are very basic, there's an easier way to get the job done.

One excellent way to sidestep complex conjugation is to use auxiliary, or helping, verbs. If you think back to English grammar classes, you may remember that a helping verb is always used with a main verb. For example, in the phrase "I do travel," the verb "do" helps the main verb "travel." The most common helping verbs in English are "be," "have," and "do." In some other languages (e.g., French or Spanish) "go" and "want" are also considered helping verbs. For example, "I want to travel." By learning how to conjugate these few verbs and use them in conjunction with main verbs, you can express many ideas in a variety of tenses and still sound relatively fluent.

For example, if you wanted to express the simple idea that you had already eaten, you would have to conjugate the verb "eat" to create the first-person past tense form meaning "I ate." The same process is required for any other verb, any other personal pronoun, and any other tense. As such, the idea that a group of people will pay for something requires you to conjugate "pay" into the future tense of the third-person plural to render "they will pay." As you might imagine, conjugation takes a lot of time and brain cells.

However, by using the magic of helping verbs, you can make your life (and your brain's life) a lot simpler. Instead of agonizing over the conjugation of "eat," you learn to conjugate the helping verb "do" and use it with the infinitive (unconjugated) form of "to eat." The result is "I *did* eat"—an easier way of conveying the same idea as "I ate." Similarly, by learning to conjugate the helping verb "to go" if it is contained in your target language and using it with the infinitive "to pay," you get, "They are going to pay."

Helping verbs really do live up to their name, so make good use of them.

Tip 17. Use specific time references to sidestep complex conjugation.

As previously explained, helping verbs can go a long way toward making you functional in a language without having to learn the complex conjugation of a large number of verbs. To make your ideas and expressions of past, present, an d future tense even clearer, you should learn some basic time references and use them in conjunction with your helping verb strategy.

Let's say you want to express the idea that you are going to leave. Using the helping verb "go" and the infinitive "to leave," you successfully express the idea "I am going to leave." That makes perfect sense, but it's still a pretty open-ended concept. Will you leave in five minutes? A week? A year? Ten years? You get the idea. Thus far, you've only established that you're not going to stay at your current location forever—a fairly unimpressive linguistic feat. By adding a simple time reference like "tomorrow" or "next week," your vague helping verb approach to the future tense suddenly becomes a very clear and meaningful statement.

With this in mind, you should make sure that you include some useful time references in your study program. In addition to specific references like "today," "yesterday," and "tomorrow," you should also learn your foreign language's patterns for saying "last," "next," "ago," and "from now." By combining these with the words for "week," "month," and "year," you can have a broad range of specific time references in your linguistic arsenal.

Tip 18. Use time particles, if applicable in your target language, to indicate completed and incomplete actions, again sidestepping complex conjugation.

One other way of avoiding (or at least minimizing) verb conjugation is to use time particles to indicate future or completed actions. Many languages that do not conjugate verbs—e.g., Thai, Vietnamese, Chinese—include these particles as an integral part of the language. In this way, the addition of a simple particle can clarify the tense of a statement by simply confirming that it has or has not yet happened.

If your target language includes these elements and doesn't require you to conjugate, you're obviously already on a roll. If it doesn't and you're sweating the conjugation thing, apply the same concept to your language by making use of the phrases "not yet" and "already." Now, instead of struggling to say "I ate," you can get by with "I eat already." Instead of "I will go," you say, "I not yet go." Although not as elegant as a perfectly conjugated or even helping verb approach, your message will still be clear. However, if you combine these terms or particles with your helping verb approach, you can have a very functional and technically accurate means of expressing tenses without having to conjugate every verb.

Tip 19. Master the basic question words—who, what, when, where, why, how, which, and how much.

One of the best ways of accelerating your study of a foreign language is to master critical basics and make them a "given." In other words, get the basics down pat so you don't have to worry about them while you're trying to achieve greater goals.

With this in mind, one of the most basic elements of any language is the interrogative group, or the question words. Just like writing an essay in school, you must have the "who," "what," "when," "where," "why," and "how" wired tight. Many languages also emphasize the concept of "which," so you should include it in your study. Also since you'll probably be shopping for something in your new language, you'll want to be sure to have the phrase "how much" down as well.

The ability to instantly recognize and use these words will go a long way toward developing your ability to ask and answer questions in your target language.

Tip 20. Avoid the temptation to use slang.

If you are over the age of 35, take a moment to listen to a teenager speaking English or to watch a few minutes of MTV. You will probably realize that although you are a native English speaker, you have little or no idea what the hell these people are saying when they use their slang. If you do understand what's being said and attempt to mimic it, you will most likely look and sound ridiculous.

Now, imagine trying to do the same thing but in a different language and with different cultural references. You will peg the ridiculous meter for sure.

The proper use of slang requires an in-depth understanding of your target language, the cultures that speak that language, and the origin and use of the slang terms themselves. In other words, unless you are absolutely sure of the meaning you are conveying, you are more likely to get in trouble or offend someone than to enhance your message through the use of slang. If you are absolutely intent on incorporating slang into your vocabulary, do lots of research and consult as many native speakers as possible before you go "live."

Tip 21. Use children's study materials in your target language to learn such basics as nouns, colors, telling time, etc.

As noted earlier, children learn languages from the ground up, mimicking the speech of adults and older children and relating spoken words directly to the objects and actions they represent. Whenever possible, this direct-relationship approach should be incorporated into your foreign language study. And one of the easiest ways to do this is by using children's books in your target language.

Children's books are usually cheaper and more user friendly than such traditional language study materials as textbooks and phrase books. They tend to be very visual and relate the subject matter directly to the target language without an intermediate English step. As such, you learn by linking the pure meaning of the material (e.g., learning colors, shapes, numbers, telling time) to the target language expressions of those concepts and ideas. In essence, you are programming yourself to think in your target language. The fact that you may also get the chance to do a little coloring never hurts either. . . .

Children's books in your target language are an inexpensive and very effective way to learn basic vocabulary. In many cases, they include only a picture or drawing and the corresponding target-language word, forcing you to make a direct association between the two and functionally think in the target language.

Tip 22. Study and learn verbs, adjectives, adverbs, and other appropriate words as antonym (opposite) pairs to make them easier to remember.

Some things just form natural pairs. The more natural something is, the easier it is to learn and remember. As such, one of the best ways to learn foreign language vocabulary is to purposely study it in antonym pairs. For example, "tall," "fast," and "large" are all easier to learn and recall if you learn them with their natural companions "short," "slow," and "small." Also, if you forget how to say one of the terms, you can still express your idea effectively by negating the other term.

Let's say you can't remember how to say "slow," but you remember the word for "fast." To express the *idea* of "slow," you simply say "not fast." Whenever possible, try to structure your study materials and curriculum to take advantage of this learning strategy.

Tip 23. Understand that dialects may affect the pronunciation and vocabulary of your target language as it is spoken in different countries or even different areas of the same country.

Once again, this is where your research into the nature of your target language pays off, because it can enable you to focus your study on the dialect or dialects that are most consistent with your goals. For example, although many textbooks and language courses are based on Castilian Spanish (the so-called "official" dialect spoken in Spain), most American Spanish speakers are more likely to come in contact with Hispanic people who speak Mexican, Cuban, Puerto Rican, or a variety of Central and South American dialects of the language. The variations between these dialects range from subtle differences in pronunciation to radical differences in terminology and even grammar.

When I studied Spanish in high school, we were required to learn the complete conjugation of each verb, which included the plural familiar, or *vosotros*, form. Years later, I was practicing Spanish with my wife, a full-blooded Mexican, and conjugated a verb to include that plural familiar form. Even though she is an educated person and a fluent speaker of her dialect of Spanish, that was literally the first time she had ever heard of that personal pronoun.

To make sure that your language study is as focused, or conversely as broad, as you would like it to be, you must become familiar with the dialects of your target languages and the differences between them. Once you understand what you're up against, you can refine your goals and, if necessary, obtain dialect-specific study materials to better achieve them.

SURROUNDING YOURSELF WITH LANGUAGE

Tip 24. Label your surroundings with your target language.

You may have noticed that one of the central strategies of my approach to foreign language study involves developing the ability to think in your target language. As mentioned previously, the idea is to eliminate the intermediate English-language step so that your thought process begins immediately with the elements of your target language. The sooner you learn to do this, the more proficient you'll become.

One way to apply this concept to common, everyday items is to physically label the objects around your house, apartment, or office to create a direct association between those objects and the target language nouns that correspond to them. In a very real way, you are surrounding yourself with your target language. The easiest way to do this is to keep a pack of Post-It notes handy as you are preparing your flash cards. When you come across a word for an easily labeled noun, prepare the sticky note and put it in place on the appropriate object.

In addition to nouns, you can also prepare notes for critical verbs. For example, if you are learning a language to apply it in a business context, in addition to a note with the word for "fax machine," you can make one with the verb "to fax" on it. Stick them both in the appropriate spot and take a moment to remind yourself of them every time you pass the fax machine.

Tip 25. Make use of idle time and make your language study spontaneous.

In a foreign country, you may not get advance warning before you have to use your language. You also won't be able to "brush up" on your vocabulary before a conversation. In other words, you'll have to use the language spontaneously. To train your mind to use your language spontaneously, you should also try to study spontaneously.

Studying spontaneously also offers other important advantages besides developing the ability to quickly "flick the switch" and turn your language skills on. One of the greatest benefits of this approach is that it allows you to reclaim lost time during your day and accomplish more. How often have you said, "I'd really like to learn how to do

_____, *but I don't have the time."* If you think of time as a block of two uninterrupted hours during your day, you're probably right. But if you look at it as a 30-minute commute each way to and from work, two 15-minute coffee breaks, 20 minutes in the waiting room of your doctor's office, and 10 minutes while you get your oil changed, you've just reclaimed two hours of study time.

The amount of time you spend isn't always as important as the consistency of your efforts. If you set aside one eight-hour day once a week to learn your language, you can get in a lot of study time. However, what happens during the six days between study times? You forget—a lot. Language study works best with consistent effort and constant review. That's what makes it "stick." As such, brief, frequent study periods are usually more productive than marathon sessions that produce little long-term retention.

So how do you make use of your idle time? By always having study materials with you. And the best materials for this task are flash cards and audiocassettes or CDs.

By keeping a stack of flash cards in your pocket or purse everywhere you go, you can instantly pull them out and sneak in some study time whenever and wherever you want. Whether it's killing a few minutes at the end of your lunch hour or passing time while you wait in line somewhere, you can keep your language study active and consistent.

If you're a rush-hour commuter, get a cassette deck in your car or bring a portable cassette player along to listen to your language tapes. If you drive alone, use the time to practice your pronunciation as well. A 30-minute commute each way to and from work means a full hour of language study five days a week. Depending on the traffic in your area, it could also be an outstanding opportunity to master and apply every curse word in your target language, as well as some choice body language.

Another tactic of spontaneous language study combines the idea of labeling the objects in your environment with the practice of talking to yourself. Let's say you need to send a fax at the office. As a diligent foreign-language student, you have already labeled the fax machine with sticky notes bearing the words that mean "fax machine" and the verb "fax." With the stage set, you walk up to the fax machine, acknowledge the vocabulary words, and then describe to yourself what you are doing as you go through the process of sending a fax. You don't need to get too elaborate, just say a few simple sentences to yourself, like "I have a fax," "I am sending a fax," and "I have sent a fax."

If you want, you can post a note that includes every conjugation for the verb "fax" and practice them all. You can pretend that you're in a foreign hotel and must ask the desk clerk to send a fax for you. You can even review your numbers by reading the phone number aloud. Use your imagination and, most important, make use of your otherwise idle time to squeeze as much language practice into your day as possible. If you do this properly, you'll dramatically increase the amount of time you spend refining your language skills. You'll also keep your study of the language much more active than the traditional classroom/homework approach.

Tip 26. Buy a shortwave radio or use Internet radio Web sites to listen to radio broadcasts in your target language.

Authentic foreign-language radio broadcasts are an excellent source of up-to-date aural comprehension material. They represent your target language the way it is actually spoken today and address current events that are usually much more interesting than the "how to buy apples" chapter of your textbook.

Thanks to the wonders of signal "skip" (a phenomenon that allows AM signals to bounce repeatedly off the Earth and the ionosphere to cover great distances), many foreign radio broadcasts can be heard hundreds or even thousands of miles from their source. Using a shortwave radio and a bit of patience, you might be able to tune in to a variety of radio broadcasts originating from countries where your target language is spoken. You can then use these live broadcasts or audio recordings of them for both active and passive study of your language.

When I was studying Vietnamese, our primary dialect was northern or Hanoi dialect because the speakers of that dialect were our primary intelligence targets. However, most of the Vietnamese speakers here in the United States were South Vietnamese who fled Vietnam after 1975. To get more practice listening to Hanoi dialect, I purchased a shortwave radio/cassette recorder and would use it to record official Vietnamese news broadcasts and the Voice of America (VOA) radio broadcasts directed at Vietnam. Later, while working in Vietnam, I also used it to bypass the propaganda they called news and listen to VOA and BBC broadcasts from outside the country.

With the advent of the Internet, there are now a wide variety of radio signals available through Web sites and Web broadcasts. With a bit of searching you should have no problem finding radio programming in your target language.

ACCELERATING YOUR
LANGUAGE STUDY WITH CULTURE

Tip 27. Learn idiomatic expressions and incorporate them into your use of the language.

Idiomatic expressions are sayings or patterns of speech that don't translate very well literally but can have very powerful meanings in a language. When used properly, they are an excellent way to demonstrate your fluency or at least create the impression that you are more fluent than you actually are.

One of my favorite examples is the Spanish phrase *En boca cerrada no entran moscas*. Literally, this means "A closed mouth lets in no flies." Idiomatically, it is the equivalent of the English expression "Silence is golden."

As you might imagine, this phrase delivered with prop-

Idiomatic expressions are a key part of every foreign language and should be included in almost every study program. Although most phrase books and language courses introduce a few of these expressions, serious linguists typically invest in dedicated idiom books like these.

er timing under the right circumstances could make you a linguistic hero, convincing the speakers around you that you have deep insight into their language and culture. Similarly, the ability to recognize and understand this phrase when it is spoken by someone else can save you a lot of confusion. With these goals in mind, learning a few select idiomatic expressions is a great way of rounding out your linguistic arsenal.

Most study materials include at least a few idiomatic expressions. Some dictionaries also address these phrases and, if you're lucky, you might even find an entire dictionary or phrase book devoted to idioms. Like spices, idioms have the best effect when used in moderation, so don't try to turn every conversation into a cliché fest. Pick a few sayings that would most likely apply to the conversational situations you anticipate most and try to keep them mentally handy so you can deliver them at the right time. As your language skills improve and you gain confidence working these into actual conversations, add more of these useful phrases to your repertoire.

Note that in addition to clever sayings, there are many other idioms used in language. Usually, these are just phrases that convey a specific meaning but typically don't translate well literally. Be on the lookout for these and learn to identify them when you hear them. If appropriate, you can ask the speaker to explain the term for you. If not, make a mental note, research it later, and add it to your active vocabulary.

One final note regarding idioms—don't try to translate English idioms literally into your target language. It doesn't work.

Think about it. You are speaking a foreign language because the people to whom you are speaking do not speak English or at least don't speak it as well as you do. With that in mind, why would you take an English idiom that would require a high level of skill in English to understand and translate it directly into their language? It sounds stupid, yet beginning linguists do it all the time—always with the same dismal results.

Remember, speaking a foreign language means playing by their rules. A bastardized hybrid language that only you understand is of no use to anyone but you.

Tip 28. Use foreign-language television broadcasts as a resource in your language training.

Audiocassettes are a great way of establishing a linguistic model for your spoken language. They are also a great way of testing your aural comprehension. However, real face-to-face conversations involve a lot more than verbal cues, so you must also learn to incorporate the visual elements of language as well.

One great way of doing this is to use foreign-language television broadcasts as a learning tool in your language study. If you have a station in your area that broadcasts regularly in your target language, turn it on and use it for both active and passive study of your language. Active study may include watching or preferably recording and analyzing programs with content that best complements your language goals. Passive study means simply having the TV tuned to that channel to get you used to hearing your language spoken constantly. You may be cleaning the house or doing other things, but one ear will at least register the presence of your target language. Subconsciously, you will also be absorbing the accent and speech patterns. Occasionally, something may really catch your ear and prompt you to pause and take a note, make a flash card, or otherwise seize that learning moment.

To satisfy basic language goals, and as part of your background research on your target language, look for children's programming that is the functional equivalent of *Sesame Street*. Like children's picture flash cards, this programming presents the fundamental elements of the language in an easily understood format. If it works for children, it will work for bigger, smarter, more literate kids like you.

If you have a satellite dish, you may have access to programming in your language that actually originates in one of the countries where it is spoken. This is a great way to prepare for a trip to that country, since it allows you to tune in on the accent, conditions, and even the current events in that area.

Speaking of current events, one excellent way of using television to practice your comprehension is to watch a news broadcast in your target language and one in English within a few hours of each other. Since the topics will be basically the same, you can compare the two and use the English broadcast to check or confirm your understanding of the foreign language one. As you get better, you may also notice the slightly different political slants of the different broadcasts and start to gain an understanding of the opinions and attitudes of the your language's culture.

As you watch TV in your target language, make an active effort to expand your understanding of the spoken language by using the context presented by the accompanying video. Ask yourself, what is the situation? What types of actions are being shown? What types of emotion are being expressed? Then, based on your answers to these questions, try to push the limits of your understanding of the spoken dialogue and "read into" the full meaning being expressed. Make sure to keep a notebook, dictionary, and blank flash cards nearby so you can record any really useful items you learn and add them to your customized curriculum.

Tip 29. Learn foreign body language and customs and incorporate them into your expression of your foreign language.

It is well known that a huge part—some say as much as 90 percent—of face-to-face communication is nonverbal. Body language, posture, facial expressions, and all the things you don't *say* actually speak volumes about the real meaning you are trying to convey.

On the positive side, this allows you to complement your spoken messages with physical gestures and expressions that can amplify and clarify your meaning. Often you can overcome shortcomings in your vocabulary and grammar through the use of body language and still get your message across clearly.

On the negative side, however, you must be aware of body language that may seem meaningless to you but carries a strong negative message in the cultures associated with your target language. For example, in Thailand it is considered very rude to show the bottoms of your feet to someone.

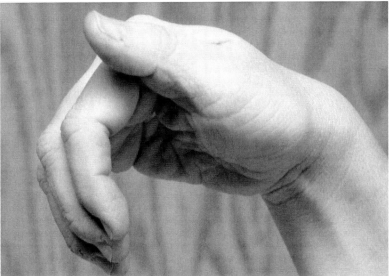

Body language is also an important part of learning a foreign language. For example, the typical one-finger method of calling someone to you used in American culture is considered rude in many other cultures. They prefer the palm-down, four-finger gesture. Including proper body language in your study curriculum will greatly improve your communication skills and possibly prevent some embarrassing moments.

When it is done intentionally, it is a huge insult. With that in mind, imagine sitting in the lobby of a nice hotel discussing business in your target language with several high-ranking executives of your parent company. Either without thinking or to consciously show them that you are at ease, you cross your legs Western style with the sole of your foot parallel to the floor. As you pivot in your seat to graciously offer eye contact to everyone, you are unintentionally giving everyone around you "the finger" (or in this case, "the foot"). Although the words you are speaking may be fluent and polite, your body language message will overshadow them.

To ensure that your body language supports your speaking skills, do some research on the culture and customs of the countries where your chosen language is spoken and consciously incorporate what you learn into your study. While watching TV programs in your target language, pay close attention to the way people carry themselves and the gestures and postures they use to support their spoken message. Then practice your foreign body language like your spoken skills and make it part of your overall effort to communicate. Even if your speaking skills come up short, you will win big points and usually come out way ahead by demonstrating polite body language and sensitivity to your language's culture.

Tip 30. Visit authentic restaurants that are culturally associated with your target language and use them as a learning resource.

One of the best ways of practicing your target language is to find a restaurant associated with one of the countries or cultures where it is spoken. Again, depending on your personal goals, try to be as specific as possible. If you are learning Spanish to go to Spain, try to find a true Spanish restaurant rather than a Mexican one.

Once inside the restaurant, determine which staff members speak your target language and start working your language into the ordering process. If the menu is labeled in both English and your target language, try to pronounce the names of the dishes in your target language and let the waiter or waitress know that you would like to practice your skills. Ask simple questions about the ordering process but don't slow the staff down. In fact, if possible, try to visit the restaurant when business is slow and the staff is more inclined to chat with you.

At the end of your first visit, tip the staff generously to acknowledge the fact that you got more than a meal for their services. Then return to the restaurant less than a week later and repeat the process. This will condition them to think of you as a "regular" and should pave the way for some à la carte language instruction. If you develop the relationship properly and they are receptive to the idea, you might be able to use the staff members to answer a variety of questions about your target language, its background cultures, idiomatic expressions, and other topics. With a bit of work, you might also be able to get them to make language practice tapes for you or provide access to other study materials.

If they aren't receptive to this idea, you should still be able to get a good handle on the ordering process and key phrases, such as the proper way of asking for the check. In the process, you can also learn what dishes you really like so you can ask for them when you travel.

Tip 31. If there is a community in your area that speaks your target language, use it as a resource to help achieve your language goals.

Immigrants from other cultures tend to settle in identifiable communities within larger municipalities. The stereotypical example of this is the "Chinatown" that seems to exist in most large cities in the United States. If such an enclave exists for speakers of your target language, you should try to identify it and use it to support your study goals.

At a basic level, you should visit the community and look

for bookstores or video stores that might sell or rent potential study resources such as dictionaries, books, magazines, newspapers, and videos. Use these to either create or supplement your courseware and to round out the resources for your personalized curriculum. Depending on your language goals, you may also be able to use these focused communities as resources to find language tutors or native speakers who can make training tapes for you, answer questions, or provide opportunities for conversational practice.

Finally, use the stores in these communities to practice shopping for and purchasing items in your target language. Even if you only buy a pack of gum, maximize the potential of that opportunity. Go into the store and greet the clerk. Ask if the store sells gum. Ask where it is and how much it costs. Pay with a larger bill so the clerk has to go through the actions of making change. Then thank the clerk and go on your way. If you do it properly, for the price of a 50-cent pack of gum you can get several minutes of private tutoring in your target language.

When I was studying Vietnamese at DLI, I made frequent visits to the Vietnamese community in San Jose, California. There I found a literal treasure trove of dictionaries and supplemental language materials that were much more up to date than the Vietnam War–era materials that formed the bulk of our formal courseware. I also had the opportunity to test my language skills with real Vietnamese speakers who were not accustomed to dealing with nonnative Vietnamese speech. I am confident that these field trips played an important part in my success in the Vietnamese program and allowed me to develop my skills far beyond those of my classmates.

Tip 32. Rent or purchase DVD movies that include foreign soundtracks in your target language and use them to practice and expand your skills.

The introduction of DVDs has revolutionized the video market. In addition to providing a truly superior video for-

SPECIAL FEATURE

- DIGITALLY MASTERED AUDIO & ANAMORPHIC VIDEO
- MASTERED IN HIGH DEFINITION
- WIDESCREEN PRESENTATION
- AUDIO: ENGLISH 5.1, FRENCH
- SUBTITLES: ENGLISH, FRENCH CHINESE, THAI
- BLACK HAWK DOWN: ON THE SET FEATURETTE
- ANIMATED MENUS
- THEATRICAL TRAILERS
- FILMOGRAPHIES
- SCENE SELECTIONS
- PRODUCTION NOTES

Special Features Not Rated

The introduction of DVD movies with soundtracks and subtitle tracks in several different languages adds a whole new element to language study. In addition to providing a tool for testing your comprehension and reading ability in your target language, they also provide insight into the proper idiomatic translation of many English phrases.

mat, DVDs also make it possible for speakers of different languages to purchase and enjoy the exact same product.

By using the multiple language tracks of DVDs, you can watch entire feature films in your target language. You can also compare the foreign-language translation of the dialogue to the English-language version—an excellent way of getting an insight into the rendering of idiomatic expressions. As you compare the two, you will notice that some ideas require more words in your target language, some require fewer words, and some do not rate a real translation at all. Once again, this is a reflection of translating the *idea* behind a situational statement rather than literally translating the words of the English dialogue. If you have a favorite movie that you've seen over and over and have practically memorized, watching it with your target-language soundtrack playing can be particularly educational because you can focus on the target-language expression of a story and dialogue that are already very familiar to you.

Some DVDs also feature subtitles in foreign languages. By changing the settings of your DVD player to display various combinations of language soundtrack and subtitles, you can mix and/or match the information to provide interesting linguistic learning experiences. One possibility is to match the tracks so you see and hear the same foreign language dialogue. If it is in fact identical (not always a guarantee), you can use the subtitles to provide the proper spelling for key terms that you might want to add to your flash card vocabulary.

If you want to challenge your reading ability, use the foreign-language subtitles like a speed-reading course, forcing you to scan the words quickly to gather the meaning. While you do this, the audio can be played in either your target language or English. For a real challenge, mute the audio and isolate the written subtitles as your only source of language input.

Tip 33. Prepare and use cheat sheets tailored to the needs of specific situational requirements.

Cheat sheets are printed, typed, or even commercially produced sheets that contain key verbs, nouns, examples of sentence structure, and other bits of information for quick and ready reference. They are the linguistic equiva-

Language cheat sheets are a great way of keeping a lot of useful language information at your fingertips. Commercial sheets like these are a good place to start, but eventually you'll want to make your own and tailor them to specific situations and environments.

lent of crib notes and can be a very useful means of keeping critical information at your fingertips.

Commercial cheat sheets, such as the Quick Study Academic sheets widely available in bookstores, are a great investment because they not only serve as useful references by themselves, but also provide an excellent model for making your own. These multicolored, multipage, laminated sheets consist of clearly defined blocks or columns of topic-specific information. For example, the first page may consist of a quick pronunciation guide, followed by a block explaining numbers, colors, common vocabulary, and useful phrases. The next page might present a conjugation guide, a list of common verbs, and a list of foods and restaurant phrases. All this information is packed into an 8 1/2 x 11 trifold outline designed to fit right into a standard three-ring binder.

Commercial cheat sheets are well worth the money; however, because your focus is a customized curriculum for your specialized needs, you'll also want to make your own. My favorite approach to portable, usable cheat sheets is to start with 5 1/2 x 8 1/2 blank note cards and, if possible, a computer and printer that will print in your target language. (Remember that Microsoft Word—probably the most commonly used word processing program—and its parent program, Office, contain a wide variety of foreign-language options. Get a good book on Office or experiment with the program's help function to learn more.) Decide which topics or situations you would like to make cheat sheets for and start compiling the information you think would be most helpful. For example, a shopping sheet might include reference blocks for numbers, colors, types of material, and such verbs as "buy," "sell," "discount," and "wrap." A restaurant cheat sheet should contain a list of your favorite foods, generic terms for "chicken," "beef," "pork," "shrimp," and, if you're really adventuresome, "eel," "goat," and "dog."

Once you've compiled your information, type it into your word processor and experiment with the font size,

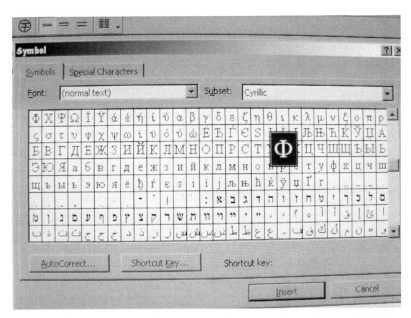

For preparing clearly printed language tools, such as cheat sheets and talking cards, remember that Microsoft Word includes many foreign-language alphabets and can even be set up for regular use in a foreign language.

page setup, and margins to create small blocks of text that can still be easily and quickly referenced. Try several different configurations for each block, making sure to include some type of descriptive label at the top of the block, and print them off on plain paper.

Now, use scissors or a paper cutter to trim the blocks to size and start laying them out like a puzzle on a note card. Try to group similar categories of information if possible and organize the information in a logical flow that will make it easy to reference. When you're happy with the layout of the first side, use a glue stick or spray adhesive to attach the paper to the card. Then flip the card over and repeat the process for the back.

Once both sides of the card are complete, buy a pack of laminating plastic from an office supply store and use it to laminate your card. For an even more professional look, take your cards to the store and have them do the laminating for you. When you're done, you'll have some very handy, topic-specific cheat sheets that you can use when operating in a foreign country.

To make the best use of these cards, keep them in your backpack or purse so you can get to them quickly when you need them. Then when you are attempting to eat at a restaurant, shop for souvenirs, or direct a taxi driver to a specific location, pull out the appropriate card and refer to it as necessary. These cards are not a substitute for language proficiency. They are simply a convenient way of ensuring that you have the linguistic tools you need when you need them.

Tip 34. For critical needs that must be communicated clearly, make dedicated "talking cards" to show to foreign speakers.

Some messages must be delivered clearly and perfectly understood by the person with whom you are communicating. For example, if you have a medical condition or serious allergy to a particular food or medicine, you don't want to take any chances. If you have a critical need to go to a hospital, doctor's office, or police station, you can't afford any miscommunication that might result in wasted time.

For critical needs such as these, your best bet is to prepare "talking cards," pocket-sized cards that contain specific printed messages in a foreign language. The idea with talking cards is to show them to a literate foreign speaker so he can read the message and understand it clearly, essentially removing the verbal element from the process.

Since talking cards must be linguistically perfect, it is best to have the exact wording of the message prepared by a native speaker of your target language who is also completely fluent in English and understands your critical need. For example, if you have a particular food allergy, it might be best to find a doctor or pharmacist who speaks your target language fluently and enlist his services to get the proper wording for the card. Even if you must pay for this service, it's worth the money and the peace of mind.

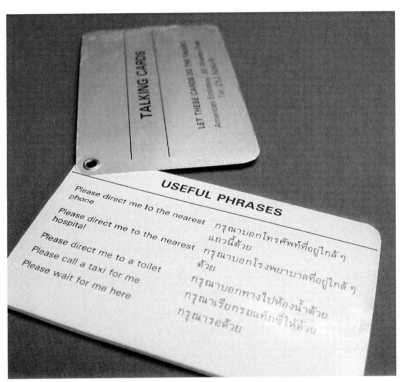

Talking cards are pocket-sized cards printed in English and a foreign language that contain critical phrases and locations. By showing these to a literate taxi driver, policeman, or other person and simply pointing to the correct phrases, you can communicate very effectively without speaking the language. These are the author's original talking cards from the U.S. Embassy in Bangkok.

If your target language does not use a romanized alphabet, have your native speaker print the messages clearly on 3 x 5–inch note cards, both in the target language and in English. Then print a corresponding romanized phonetic version on the opposite side of the card so you can amplify your message verbally as a person reads it. This also provides a verbal backup plan in case the person to whom you are speaking—like a taxi driver or food-service person—can't read.

The idea for talking cards came from the U.S. Embassy

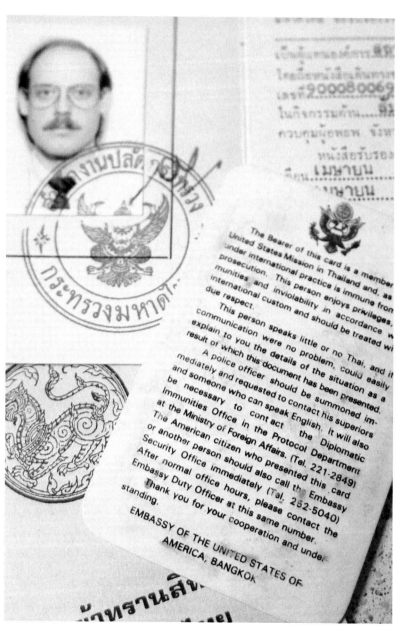

The Bearer of this card is a member of the United States Mission in Thailand and, as under international practice is immune from prosecution. This person enjoys privileges, immunities and inviolability in accordance with international custom and should be treated with due respect.

This person speaks little or no Thai, and if communication were no problem, could easily explain to you the details of the situation as a result of which this document has been presented.

A police officer should be summoned immediately and requested to contact his superiors and someone who can speak English. It will also be necessary to contact the Diplomatic Immunities Office in the Protocol Department at the Ministry of Foreign Affairs. (Tel. 221-2849) The American citizen who presented this card or another person should also call the Embassy Security Office immediately (Tel. 252-5040) After normal office hours, please contact the Embassy Duty Officer at this same number. Thank you for your cooperation and understanding.

EMBASSY OF THE UNITED STATES OF AMERICA, BANGKOK

Here's the ultimate talking card—the "get out of jail free" card issued to many diplomatic mission members in foreign countries.

in Bangkok, Thailand. As part of the in-processing procedure, each newly assigned person was given a welcome kit that included a pack of talking cards. Actually, the pack was connected by a grommet that kept all the cards together, but allowed you to pivot them to expose the desired message. For folks new to Thailand, these cards were an excellent tool for communicating with taxi drivers and getting around town while they developed a feel for the spoken language. Although I spoke some Thai when we first arrived, I traveled a lot and was frequently away from home. My wife, an extremely resourceful and adventuresome person, used our Thai talking cards with great effect and explored much of Bangkok during my absence.

Another application of this concept was the U.S. State Department's "get out of jail free" card. This plastic card contained an official printed statement in both Thai and English that explained that the bearer was a member of the U.S. diplomatic mission and enjoyed "privileges, immunities, and inviolability in accordance with international custom and should be treated with due respect." Needless to say, when that particular talking card spoke, people listened.

Tip 35. Whenever possible, pick up business cards in the native language for your hotel, office, favorite restaurants, and businesses located near major landmarks.

The idea behind this strategy is to use business cards printed in your target foreign language (and preferably English, as well) as a type of talking card. Most major hotels and foreign businesses print their cards so that they include both an English and native-language version of the information on the card. If they have separate cards in each language, get one of each and staple them together to create a bilingual card.

When you are ready to go somewhere, pull out the appropriate card and show it to the taxi driver to clearly

Make a habit of picking up business cards for your hotel, office, and favorite restaurants that are printed in your target language. By showing a taxi driver the card and mastering a simple phrase like "Please take me here," you can get around in a foreign city very effectively.

establish your desired destination. Then complete the process with a few simple spoken phrases like "How much to go to this place?" or "Please take me here," and you'll be on your way.

This is an excellent tactic for businessmen who must travel often but don't spend enough time in any one country to justify in-depth language study. To make this tactic even more effective, combine your use of the business cards with a taxi-oriented cheat sheet containing a pronunciation guide, a crash course in numbers and currency, and a few simple phrases to get the taxi rolling in the right direction.

If you are traveling somewhere for the first time, call the business you will be visiting (or ask the desk clerk at your hotel to do so) and have a representative fax you a copy of the firm's native-language business card. That will get you there the first time so you can pick up a real business card for your collection. If you use this tactic a lot, laminate your favorite cards so they last longer.

Tip 36. Learn how to give simple directions to a taxi driver so you can direct him to places you know.

In general, local taxi drivers usually know their way around better than you; however, there may be many times when they don't know the exact final destination you have in mind. In such instances, you should first have the ability to describe a major landmark near your desired location. This can be a hotel, a well-known tourist spot, a shopping center, or a major street intersection. You should then describe in general terms where your desired location is in relation to the landmark. To do this, you need to learn to use words and phrases like "near," "across from," "behind," and "next to" to give the driver a general reference.

Once you're in the vicinity of the major landmark, you should have the ability to "talk your driver in" to your exact destination. By using simple directions such as "go straight," "turn left," "turn right," "slow down," "we're almost there," and "stop here," you can easily direct him where you want to go.

When I lived in Bangkok the first time, I quickly grew tired of hotel life and rented a house with an air force buddy of mine. Unlike the hotel, which was located on a major street, our house was about a mile and at least half a dozen zigzag turns from the nearest major road. To get there by taxi, I first cited the major street reference and the intersection of the nearest cross street to get the driver in the ballpark and negotiate a fare (this was before metered taxis became popular in Bangkok). When we got near the referenced intersection, I explained that my actual destination was near that intersection and that he'd have to go a little farther. Once we hit the intersection, I simply talked him through each turn with simple commands until we got where I was going.

This approach is also an excellent way to learn to give

Learning how to give simple directions in your target language can get you to nontourist destinations, such as this one in Cairo, Egypt—or prevent you from being taken to them against your will.

directions in your target language because it allows you to practice formulating step-by-step instructions and relating them to street names and landmarks.

Tip 37. Use maps labeled in English and your target language to help you get around and to direct taxi drivers.

Maps that are small enough to be handy, yet detailed enough to get you where you're going can also be an excellent tool when navigating foreign countries. Since they combine specific place names with visual references for streets, landmarks, and directions, they can go a long way toward amplifying your expression of the target language and your understanding of a native speaker's directions. When working with taxi drivers, a map also lets your driver know that you are at least somewhat familiar with the geography of the area. This reduces the chances of your being "taken for a ride"—driven all over town to jack up the price of what was really a short-distance trip or, even worse, driven somewhere you really don't want to go, where you might meet some of his friends you really don't want to know.

I used maps regularly when traveling in major Vietnamese cities, such as Hanoi and Saigon, to make sure I was going where I wanted to go. In Manila, even though I did all my negotiating in English, I typically carried a map to communicate to the driver that I knew—or at least could track—my way around town. This was important because it was common for drivers of metered taxis to attach the meter to their car horn instead of the odometer. Rather than every tenth of a mile, as it should have, the meter would advance each time the horn was blown—a common occurrence in Manila traffic. By flashing the map and negotiating a flat rate (that the driver could pocket without having to declare it against his meter total), I always got where I was going for a fair price and never had to deal with any taxi-related ambushes.

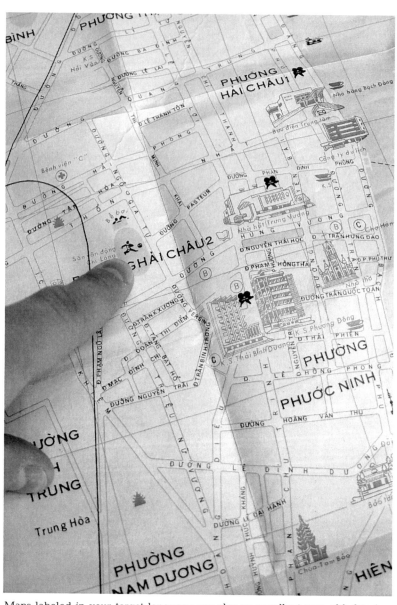

Maps labeled in your target language are also an excellent way of bolstering your speaking skills to clearly communicate where you want to go. They also let your driver know that you know your way around a bit, making it less likely that you'll be "taken for a ride."

Tip 38.   Use native speakers as living dictionaries to answer questions and enhance your language skills.

In a foreign country, you will obviously be surrounded by your target language and have the opportunity to practice speaking, listening, and reading as much as you want. To make the most of it, however, you should use it and the help of native speakers to fill in the blanks in your customized curriculum. Instead of creating targeted study materials by reading a book or looking up words in a dictionary, learn to ask questions to satisfy specific linguistic goals.

Two of the most useful questions you can learn to ask are "What is this called in (your target language)?" and, for native speakers who understand some English, "How do I say _____ in (your target language)?" To use the former, point to or pick up the object and say your line. For the latter, you must have already established that the speaker knows some English so he will recognize the English term you are trying to translate.

Once you get more proficient at your target language, you can use native speakers as dictionaries and language coaches by describing a situation to them and then asking what phrase or statement would be most appropriate in that situation. For example, to learn the proper, idiomatic way to ask for the check in a restaurant, you could describe the situation in your target language. You might say something like, "I have just finished eating at a restaurant and want to pay. What do I say to the waiter?"

Because of the differences in social class and their effects on formal and informal speech, it is always a good idea to ask several people your question and cross-reference their answers. Similarly, you should check their answers against dictionaries and other resources to ensure that you are saying what you want the way you want to say it. In some cases, their answer may be appropriate for them as locals and at their social status yet entirely inappropriate for a foreigner operating in polite company. In other cases, they may give you an incorrect answer as a joke.

When I was working in Haiphong, Vietnam, my team stayed at a very nice (in other words, reasonably rat-free) hotel on the Do Son Peninsula. This area is one of the more scenic places in northern Vietnam, and the staff at the hotel was convinced that it would someday become a popular destination for foreign tourists. As such, they asked me and the other linguist on my team to teach them some situational English. Specifically, they wanted to know how to greet a guest passing through the lobby, invite him to sit down, and ask him for a drink order. In the spirit of small-time Cold War politics, the phrasing we taught them was, "Hey, you! Sit your ass down. What the f#^k do you want to drink?"

To their credit, within a few days they were delivering these lines like pros. Trusting us was functionally a mistake. Be aware that the same could happen to you and cross-check your answers before you start repeating phrases taught to you by locals.

Tip 39. Carry a portable cassette recorder with you when traveling in foreign countries and use it to record conversations with native speakers, airport announcements, and anything else you'd like to analyze or practice.

Sometimes things just happen too quickly for you to keep up. The next best thing to stopping time to allow you to think is the ability to *replay* time so you can analyze it more closely. One of the best ways to do this is to use your handy pocket recorder to record such things as bus, train, and airport announcements, specific conversations with native speakers, or any other situational speech that you'd like to analyze in greater detail. This will give you the opportunity to replay the speech and analyze it at your own pace until you decipher its format and meaning.

For example, you are far off the beaten path, waiting

for your train to be announced at the terminal. All the announcements are made only in your target language, so there's no English soundtrack to fall back on. To make sure you don't miss your train, record a few announcements for other trains and play them back to determine the format of the announcement and the key vocabulary terms. Once you realize that all the announcements are structured the same (e.g., the train number, followed by its scheduled time, final destination, and track number), you'll be much better prepared to recognize and understand the announcement for your train.

Once you get on the train, you might do the same thing to get a handle on the conductor's announcements so you don't miss your stop.

As noted earlier, recording conversations with native speakers can also be a great way of learning new vocabulary and speech patterns, as well as grading your linguistic performance and accent. Video camcorders are also great for this purpose since they will allow you to capture body language, written signs, and other visual cues to complement the audio. One word of caution, however—be careful recording or photographing anything in communist countries or places experiencing a lot of political tension. Also, avoid photographing or videotaping soldiers and policemen. Although you may have the best of intentions, they won't necessarily see it that way and may choose to see you as a spy rather than an aspiring linguist.

Tip 40. Remember that the ultimate goal in any language is effective communication. Learn to supplement your verbal skills with appropriate physical gestures and the use of visual aids to get the job done.

Applying your language in a foreign country is outcome-based education at its best. As long as you can get the right message across at the right time and get what you want out of the deal, you're on a roll. With that in mind, learn to use the strategies in this book, your environment, and your own imagination to create a total communication package based on your abilities in your target language.

I remember working with a veteran linguist in Vietnamese who was, for lack of a better term, a legend in his own mind. His real, usable skills in Vietnamese were nowhere close to what he claimed to be able to do. One day we were working at the Green Island Detention Center, a small island in Hong Kong harbor where newly arrived Vietnamese "asylum seekers" received their initial processing into Hong Kong's refugee system. For most of the morning, we happily shared an interview room and worked side by side. When I ran out of folks to interview, my "colleague," who appeared to be having a bit of trouble with his subject, asked me to leave the room. Being a good intel guy, I stepped out of the room just far enough to see and hear what was going on without his seeing me. It turned out that there were two reasons for his request for privacy. First, he was collecting information that was more closely related to my mission requirements than his so that he could claim credit for more interviews. Second, he was having a hell of a time trying to phrase the questions necessary to conduct the interview properly. Once I left the room, his "interview" quickly mutated into a game of Vietnamese charades, in which he physically acted out various scenarios and allowed the interviewee to pick the most correct version.

To this day, I still don't have a great deal of respect for my former colleague or his abilities. However, I do have to give him credit for showing me how much communication can actually be achieved with meager verbal skills and a good dose of theatrics.

On a less dramatic scale, one excellent way of maximizing your communication skills—especially when shopping—is to bring along an electronic calculator. If your language skills should happen to come up short during a negotiation, or if you just want to confirm that what you're hearing is actually what the vendor expects you to pay, use the calculator to fill in the blanks. In many Asian markets, vendors have embraced this idea and reduced price negotiation to a ritual that consists of pointing at the item or items you want to buy, punching numbers into the calculator to indicate the suggested price, and then passing the calculator back and forth to allow both buyer and seller to enter counter offers. When both sides finally agree on a price, the head shakes, frowns give way to nods and smiles, and the deal is sealed.

Calculators also come in handy for figuring currency exchange rates and maintaining (or at least assessing the damage of) your travel budget, so they can be a very useful part of your travel kit.

Tip 41.   Understand that even though humor is a universal concept enjoyed by all cultures, most jokes do not translate very effectively from one language to another.

Did you ever wonder why we use the term "sense" of humor? It's because everyone interprets and evaluates humor on a different scale, based on their culture, their values, and the quality and spirit of the joke itself.

Like using slang, telling a joke in a foreign language requires an in-depth understanding of the language itself and the many cultural nuances that might affect the interpretation of your attempt at humor. Even if you get to a level where you have this kind of insight, you still have to be capable of actually being funny—a quality that completely eludes some people in all languages.

For the most part, you should avoid the temptation to tell jokes in your target language. If you can't, either stick to repeating jokes that you've heard from native speakers or learn to make up jokes based on the terms of the foreign culture. For example, the Vietnamese have a style of joking called *nói lái*, which translates roughly as "speaking back slang." Vietnamese words consist of three basic parts: an initial sound, an ending sound, and a tone. In this type of humor, you try to think of a two-word compound that has a normal meaning, but when you switch the ending sounds of the two words (keeping the initial sound and tone the same), you get a very different, hopefully humorous, meaning. Although it has no direct English equivalent, if you think of the term "bass-ackwards" representing the real meaning "ass-backwards," you're on the right track.

At the height of my Vietnamese language skills, I actually became pretty adept at this game and even learned how to strategically work it into conversations to increase its effect. My crowning achievement was an incredibly clever statement in which the Vietnamese term for "four lanterns" served as a not-so-veiled reference to cunnilingus. I knew immediately that I had succeeded in my efforts at humor when a Vietnamese bar girl blew almost half a beer through her nose.

One final word on humor—no matter what you do, do not try to literally translate an English-language joke into a foreign language. With very, very few exceptions, it does not work. And being unfunny in two languages is even worse than bombing in just one.

MASTERING THE WRITTEN FORM OF YOUR LANGUAGE

Tip 42. Practice tracing foreign-language alphabets before you attempt to write them on blank paper.

As I explained earlier in this book, many languages do not have standard romanized alphabets. If your goals include learning how to read and write using a foreign writing system, practice tracing the characters before you try writing them.

Let's face it: writing is a complex motor skill. To master complex motor skills, you need lots of quality repetition of that skill. And the easiest way to achieve such repetition is by redoing something that you know is already right.

To learn to write using a nonromanized alphabet or character-based writing system, you should first learn the basic letters and the order of the pen strokes necessary to write them properly. Remember, learning a language means learning by its rules, so don't try to invent your own stroke order or do things your own way. There is a method to their madness. Usually, it determines the look and legibility of true handwritten (as opposed to hand-*printed*) text. If your stroke order is wrong, the letters/characters won't look right when you try to write quickly.

Once you have a basic understanding of the mechanics of writing your new alphabet, photocopy several pages of text in your target language and practice tracing over the letters on the photocopy. Doing this repeatedly will get you used to the proper order of the strokes and the size and scale of the different parts of the characters. If necessary, use the photocopier to enlarge your source text until it is the size of normal handwritten words.

After you've developed some muscle memory and are comfortable tracing the letters, alternate between tracing and actually writing. Place the photocopy and a blank sheet of paper side by side. Trace a letter or entire word to get a feel for its written form and then immediately write the word on the blank sheet of paper. Compare the two and repeat as necessary until your handwriting has the proper form.

Used properly, this method will have you writing faster and more legibly than the traditional copying technique.

Tip 43. Use the shape and design of foreign-language words and characters to offer visual cues to their meanings.

Chinese characters originated as true pictograms: artistic shorthand for the objects and actions they represented. Through the centuries, they evolved into a simpler and less visually suggestive form; however, they still contain visual cues that can give an insight into their meaning. For example, the Chinese-Mandarin word for "liquor" is *jiu*. In its ancient form, it started off as a drawing of a jar. As the language evolved, the drawing was represented more simplistically, and the radical (a key element suggesting the meaning of a character) for water was added to indicate the jar is full. By understanding this evolution, the resulting modern character is easier to recognize and remember.

Chinese characters are unique in that they are not an alphabet. Each one has a distinct meaning, and both this meaning and the pronunciation of the symbol must be learned by rote. Because of their origin, they are particularly visual and symbolic in nature. However, that doesn't mean that this strategy is limited to the study of Chinese.

If you are learning a language with a nonromanized alphabet, spend some time looking at the visual structure of the words when you're doing

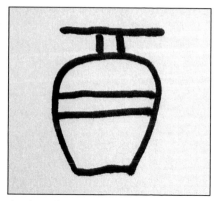

Ancient pictogram meaning "jar."

Simplified symbol for "jar."

Modern Chinese character for "liquor."

your flash card practice. With a little imagination, you will start to see visual cues and hints within the form of the words that can help you remember their meanings. Like anything that involves imagination and vision, this is a very individual thing. As with finding constellations in the sky, one person may see symbolism in a written word that another person can't. That's okay. As long as what you see works for you, you're good to go.

Tip 44. Practice transcribing sentences read aloud or played from audiotape to ensure that you can accurately hear every word.

Like English, many languages have homonyms—words that sound alike but have different meanings. In English, these words usually sound identical but are spelled differently: "through" and "threw" or "there," "their," and "they're." To differentiate between these words, we need to hear them in context. By using the other words in the sentence to understand the general meaning, we can discern the specific meaning of the word in question.

In other languages homonyms can be much more challenging. In tonal languages, such as Thai and Vietnamese, two words can be spelled exactly alike yet have different tones or inflections. These tones are in fact an integral element of every word and, in the mind of a native speaker, make two seemingly similar words distinctly different.

In Chinese, the plot thickens further because many characters with distinctly different meanings share the same pronunciation—including the tone. In many cases, the only way to determine the meaning of a word is to see it written or to define it as part of a two-character compound, using the meaning of the other character to suggest the meaning of the one in question.

To challenge your ability to hear every word in a sentence and differentiate between homonyms, you should incorporate transcription into your language practice. When you first start out, use prerecorded language tapes from a formal course that includes a book or workbook with the correct written versions of the sentences. Listen to each sentence on the tape and write it in your target language. Once you've completed all the sentences, check your answers.

As your knowledge of the language gets better, you can record your own language tapes, have a native speaker do it for you, or even try your hand at transcribing portions of radio and TV broadcasts. If you doubt the accuracy of your transcription, have it checked by a native speaker or simply look up the words in question to make sure that your transcribed version actually makes sense.

Transcription practice is also an excellent way to challenge yourself to "listen through" the slurred words, speech impediments, accents, static, and ambient noise that plague most recording formats. With practice, you learn to fill in the blanks in a spoken sentence, divining its meaning from context even though you really didn't hear every word spoken.

ADVANCED STUDY CONCEPTS AND STRATEGIES

Tip 45. Keep building your reference library and always be on the lookout for books, dictionaries, and other resources that you can use to expand your knowledge of the target language.

The higher you set your linguistic goals, the more tools you'll need to achieve them. As such, you should always be on the lookout for new reference and study materials. If you travel to foreign countries where your target language is spoken, you should budget some time during every trip to visit at least one bookstore. Trips to areas that include appropriate cultural centers and universities should also include some time for research and book shopping.

If you use your language to address very specific topics, you should look for specialized dictionaries dedicated to those topics and add them to your personal reference library.

Always look for opportunities to expand your library of foreign language reference materials. Although such materials usually take the form of dictionaries, books, and magazines, they can also include other items such as the leaflets shown at top. Note the use of simple visual messages to amplify the meaning of the written text in the leaflets.

When I was working in the intelligence field, I had the good fortune to befriend a spook who specialized in acquiring foreign-language reference materials for our government. These materials were typically published in foreign countries and very difficult to obtain outside those countries. Once we had an original of one of these, his government agency would reprint it and distribute it throughout the intelligence community for reference use. Unfortunately this usually took at least a year.

During my travels in Vietnam, I stopped at every book-store I could find and bought multiple copies of every good reference book they had. One of these was always ear-marked for my friend, who reciprocated by giving me special priority on his distribution list. Within a couple of years, I had a better Vietnamese reference library than some government agencies.

Tip 46. Use your knowledge of one language to help you learn other languages.

Languages are typically classified into families (e.g., Germanic languages, Romance languages). The languages within a particular family share similar origins and therefore are similar in sound and structure. In most cases, they also share many cognates that make developing a useful vocabulary very easy. As such, knowledge of one language in a family can make it much easier to learn another language in that family. For example, a Spanish speaker would have a much easier time learning Portuguese than a person with no previous language background.

Even if your current language background and your target language are very different, previous linguistic experience can still give you an important edge. Even though two languages may be from different linguistic families, they may share certain traits or phonetic elements that are similar to each other but very different from English. In such cases, you can borrow what you need from a language you already know to help you learn something new.

If you study more than one language, it is often possible to use your knowledge and experience in one language to help you learn another. The author used these books, designed to teach Thai and Khmer to native Vietnamese speakers, to accelerate his study of these other languages. Since the phonetic sounds and grammar patterns of these languages are more similar to each other than to English, knowledge of Vietnamese was a great head start.

When I was learning Thai, I was already proficient in Vietnamese. Although these two languages have different roots and belong to different linguistic families, they do share a number of sounds that do not exist in English. For new speakers of either language, learning these unusual sounds is very challenging and time consuming. However, since I was already familiar with Vietnamese phonetics, I was able to borrow the necessary sounds from Vietnamese to accurately pronounce words in Thai. In fact, I based all my Thai notes and flash cards on the Vietnamese alphabet (which is already in a functionally romanized form) rather than the romanized phonetic system that was the standard in our textbooks.

Later, I even found books designed to teach native

Vietnamese speakers how to speak Thai. In addition to the standard English-to-Thai approach I took in my formal training, I supplemented my study by approaching Thai through the eyes (and ears) of a Vietnamese speaker. Using the parallels and comparisons in these books, I was able to use my knowledge of Vietnamese to significantly enhance and accelerate my study of Thai, achieving functional results in a very short time.

Tip 47. Whenever possible, practice speaking your target language on the telephone.
As noted elsewhere, in face-to-face communication, it is possible to use body language and your environment to enhance your verbal skills and maximize your chances of communicating effectively. However, once you become somewhat proficient in your language of choice, you should try removing those visual elements from your communication to challenge your pure verbal skills. With nothing visual to fall back on, you will have to express everything verbally and make sure that your spoken communication is perfectly clear and logical.

In addition to providing an additional challenge, using the telephone is also an opportunity for you to learn about the nuances of phone etiquette and vocabulary in your target language. For example, the standard greeting used when answering the phone in Thailand translates to "Where are you?" rather than the expected "Hello." This is because in the early days of the Thai phone system, telephones were not located in individual homes but in key public places. As such, all phone calls were made from one *place* to another before they were made from one person to another. The place reference stuck and continues to this day.

Another advantage of using the phone in your foreign language is that it prevents the other person from seeing who you are. If your verbal skills and accent are good enough, you can actually try passing as a native speaker. While I was working in Vietnam in the early 1990s, many hotels (especially the nasty ones we typically stayed in) only had a single phone at the front desk. I often asked the hotel staff if I could answer the phone for them to see if the caller could recognize me as a nonnative speaker. I eventually got to the point that I could easily pass for a native Vietnamese speaker for at least several minutes before the caller noticed anything nonnative about my speech pattern.

Aside from the feeling of accomplishment this gave me, my near-native accent also gave me an important advantage when shopping. One of the more desirable items in Vietnamese marketplaces (at least for me) was genuine Havana Club rum. Unfortunately, like most things in Vietnam, the price of this item varied according to the buyer's nationality. Since Americans, Canadians, and Western Europeans had more money, the Vietnamese typically charged us more money than they would a fellow Vietnamese consumer.

To overcome this challenge, I developed the tactic of hiding just out of sight of the shop merchant and waiting until he was busy doing something. I would then step up and quickly ask the price of the rum in my best Vietnamese accent. If I got lucky—which happened about half the time—he would answer with the "local" price before he saw that I was not Vietnamese. Once the price was stated, he was committed, and I got some very good rum at a very good price.

Tip 48. Learn as much as you can about the culture, customs, and history of the countries where your target language is spoken.

As I've stated previously, every language is a direct reflection of the cultures that created it. The deeper your understanding of these cultures, their customs, and their history, the greater insight you'll have into their language.

This is particularly true when you look at the meanings of idiomatic expressions. For example, a common greeting in Vietnamese translates literally as "Have you eaten yet?" Greetings are typically expressions of courtesy and concern for the welfare of others. In this case, it reflects a concern that one's neighbor might not have enough to eat—a concern that is prevalent in countries that have experienced famine and starvation.

One quick and interesting way of getting an insight into a country's culture is to look at the images on its currency. Third-world countries with currencies featuring pictures of tractors and combines obviously have slightly different cultural priorities than countries that prefer images of famous statesmen or national landmarks.

Studying the history, culture, and customs related to your language will also give you the insight to communicate using proper body language and other nonverbal means.

Tip 49. Analyze music in your target language to learn how to express ideas creatively and poetically.

Because of its lyrical nature, music presents a special challenge to the aspiring linguist. In most cases, song lyrics do not consist of everyday conversational vocabulary and focus on metaphors and poetic terms. Even if a song consists of common words, the timing and tempo of their delivery is usually much different from conversational speech and therefore harder to understand.

As an advanced linguist, you should listen to at least some music in your target language and try to understand both its literal and figurative meanings. In addition to giving you yet another insight into the culture behind your chosen language, it will also give you a feel for how your target language can be used to express ideas creatively and poetically. Also, as with idiomatic expressions, you never know when a few well-chosen song lyrics might come in handy.

At the end of a month-long investigative mission in northern Vietnam, my team and I returned to Hanoi to finish our written reports and prepare for our return to

Thailand. Although our hotel was a typical, dismal North Vietnamese structure, it was staffed by about half a dozen young, attractive Vietnamese girls. Despite orders that strictly forbade any kind of fraternization with Vietnamese nationals, a member of my team made a rather awkward attempt at scoring some intimate female companionship by offering one of the girls a deck of playing cards in return for sexual favors.

Once I became aware of the problem, I confined the team member to his room and apologized to the girl in question. To restore her faith in Americans and ensure that the incident didn't escalate into a larger problem, I explained in my best Vietnamese that every culture has good people and bad people, and that most of the members of my team—and by extension most Americans— were in fact good people.

Impressed with my efforts to explain the more esoteric aspects of human nature to her in Vietnamese, she asked if I had ever tried writing poetry in Vietnamese. I explained that I hadn't but, to make her feel better, I would give it a try.

After a few minutes of feigned thought, I wrote down several lyrics from a song written by a U.S.-based Vietnamese band. Since such music had not yet filtered back to Vietnam, it was a pretty good bet that she had not heard the song. To make a long story short, I quickly established myself as both a sensitive, caring guy and a poetic genius among all the girls at the hotel. Had I not been happily married and operating under strict fraternization rules, I would have also had a much better chance of finding love than propositioning girls with playing cards.

Tip 50. "Don't judge the whole world by your own shitty standards."

This is actually a favorite quote of mine from my friend James Keating, one of the most talented martial arts practitioners and instructors in the United States. In essence, it means that if you choose to do a poor job of something, you should not expect the rest of the world to lower its standards to meet yours.

Applying this concept to language, if you choose to do a half-hearted job of learning a language and manage to get by with poor skills and a lousy accent, you haven't accomplished much. Even if you manage to get around town, order food and drinks, and function reasonably well, the fact remains that you have poor language skills and a lousy accent.

To understand this more clearly, think of a newly arrived Pakistani cab driver in New York City or any other nonnative English speaker whom you've had to struggle to understand. His English is terrible, but you manage to decipher his words and hammer home your own to ultimately get what you want. In all fairness, most of the credit in that situation goes to you as the listener.

Putting the shoe on the other foot, if you manage to get things done with lousy foreign language skills, most of the credit for that accomplishment should not go to you but to the people who struggled to understand you. For example, most of the "fluent" speakers I've met in bars in Thailand are readily understood only because the Thais who work there are so used to having their language butchered by drunken foreigners.

From the outset, I said that this book is geared toward helping you achieve your personal language goals. You must understand, however, that there is a big difference between setting simple goals and accepting low standards. If after reading this book and considering all the strategies herein you decide to learn only one phrase in a foreign language, fine. Please just learn it well.